Swing Trading:

How to swing Trade For a Living With Proper Money Management, Psychology, Secrets And Proven Swing Strategies To Trade With Options, Stocks And Forex. 7-Days Crash Course For Beginners

ROBERT ZONE

Table of Contents

Introduction

Chapter 1 Basics of Swing Trading

Chapter 2 How Swing Trading Works?

Chapter 3 Platforms And Tools For Trading

Chapter 4 Financial Instruments for Swing Trading

Chapter 5 Candlestick Chart Patterns and Technical Indicators

Chapter 6 Swing Trading Rules

Chapter 7 Fundamental and Technical Analysis

Chapter 8 Money Management

Chapter 9 Swing Trading Strategies

Conclusion

© **Copyright 2019 - All rights reserved.**

The content contained within this book may not be reproduced, duplicated or transmitted without direct written permission from the author or the publisher.

Under no circumstances will any blame or legal responsibility be held against the publisher, or author, for any damages, reparation, or monetary loss due to the information contained within this book. Either directly or indirectly.

Legal Notice:

This book is copyright protected. This book is only for personal use. You cannot amend, distribute, sell, use, quote or paraphrase any part, or the content within this book, without the consent of the author or publisher.

Disclaimer Notice:

Please note the information contained within this document is for educational and entertainment purposes only. All effort has been executed to present accurate, up to date, and reliable, complete information. No warranties of any kind are declared or implied. Readers acknowledge that the author is not engaging in the rendering of legal, financial, medical or professional advice. The content within this book has been derived from various sources. Please consult a licensed professional before attempting any techniques outlined in this book.

By reading this document, the reader agrees that under no circumstances is the author responsible for any losses, direct or indirect, which are incurred as a result of the use of information contained within this document, including, but not limited to, — errors, omissions, or inaccuracies.

Introduction

Swing trading enables you to take advantage of changes in stock prices, also known as swings to make profit. The strategy presents you with numerous benefits that are missing in both day trading as well as buy and hold investment strategies. You can make profit from both the upward and downward changes in stock prices.

As a swing trader, you can trade several instruments including stocks, options, futures and currencies. This book discusses numerous components of swing trading and teaches you how to swing trade the numerous financial instruments mentioned above. It defines the trading style and outline the basics involved in the trade. It also highlights the advantages and disadvantages of swing trading different types of stocks and options.

The book also provides you information on the tools and platforms necessary for swing trading and highlights the strategies beginners as well as professional traders can employ to succeed in the trade.

As you scan through the book, you will get to understand how to determine entry and exit points for each trade, as well as how to minimize the risks associated with the trade. The book covers all the latest topics associated with swing trading and lists some of the ways you can use to analyze the swing market for the best opportunities. If you read the whole of it, you will master every skill required to excel as a swing trader. Ideally this books is great addition to your library whether you are a new trader or an expert swing trader seeking to diversify your portfolio.

Swing trading represents an exciting opportunity for those who are interested in trading and going beyond the normal method of buying stock and holding it. And yet, many of those same people find the idea of day trading to be too extreme. We will begin the book with a discussion of the fundamentals of swing trading. We will introduce the concept, which is actually quite simple. We will discuss the advantages of swing trading and talk about risk management. We will also compare and contrast it with day trading.

Then we will talk about following a trend, which is one of the most lucrative ways to make money while swing trading. After this, we will introduce the main tools that are used by swing traders including technical indicators like Bollinger bands, and we will also discuss candlestick charts.

Then we will talk about using swing trading with the many different financial securities that are available today. This will include a discussion of swing trading stocks, which is where most people swing trade. We will also talk about using swing trading on the foreign exchange markets, swing trading with the exchange-traded funds, and will also discuss options and crypto. We will close out the book with a discussion of the psychology of swing trading in the best tools and platforms to use, including finding the right broker.

Chapter 1   Basics of Swing Trading

Before you get into swing trading, you want to ensure that it is the right trading strategy for you. You already know the basic definition of swing trading, so now it is time to discuss what makes it special. Swing trading is a mix of other basic trading strategies. It isn't as fast-paced and stressful as scalping or day trading, but it also isn't as slow as position trading. Swing trading is perfect for anyone who wants to turn to the stock market for their career but wants to see larger profits and stay active throughout the day.

If you are comfortable with overnight risk, swing trading might be right for you. The reason why holding stocks overnight is risky is because you never know what they are going to do during the 12 or so hours you are away from your desk. The price of stocks can fall quickly, which means you can have a good standing with the stock when you close out at 4:00 P.M. on Tuesday. However, at 8:30 A.M. on Wednesday morning, you can find out the price of your stock fell due to shocking news about the company and now you have lost money. Of course, this risk increases when you hold stocks over the weekend.

Swing trading is unique because you are able to take time to research the history of the stock, which means you will look at its daily and weekly charts in order to find a pattern. This pattern will tell you when the best time to buy and sell your stock will be. You also have time to go through the news and get an idea of how the stock market is doing every day. You can spend time looking at various stocks to see which ones are the best for you. When trading strategies move faster than swing trading, you aren't able to spend as much time on these factors.

Swing traders have a variety of options for trading. While many people focus on individual stocks, you can also purchase a basket of stocks. This is a large group of shares, such as 100, that you buy for one price. Each share comes from a different company. You can also trade cryptocurrencies such as bitcoin.

Various Financial Instruments

While most people think of stocks when they are looking into trading, there are other financial instruments that you can focus on. Even if you use these instruments in a different market, such as Forex, you can still be a swing trader. Hence, you want to ensure that you understand what financial instrument you want to trade before you take your first step into trading.

Stocks

When discussing the stock market, this book focuses on stocks. In fact, you have already learned a lot of information about the stock market. Because of this, I won't spend a lot of time discussing stocks as a financial instrument.

Exchange-Traded Funds (ETFs)

ETFs are becoming increasingly popular and known as a basket of stocks, bonds, or other securities. People often make ETFs by combining various stocks from the market. This is helpful for several reasons. First, it gives you dozens of companies, sometimes in the hundreds, with one purchase. Because the stocks are smaller than individual stocks you would purchase, ETFs are a decent price.

Second, they are known to help limit risk. This happens because the securities in the ETFs will often balance each other out. For example, if you have a blue-chip stock, it will balance out any stocks that are performing poorly.

Third, ETFs can help people who can't watch the news as often as they would like to. This might be because they only trade part-time and don't have the ability to pay close attention to the stock market. While you will still want to do your thorough research just the same as any other stock, if one of your stocks receives bad news, you don't have to hurry to sell it. Instead, one of the other higher-performing stocks will help balance out your ETF.

Fourth, ETFs can automatically help with diversification. This is when you have a variety of companies and securities in your portfolio. It can help increase your knowledge of the market and often gives you a stronger look as a trader. The trick is you need to find the right level of diversification when using individual financial instruments as too many can be harmful to your portfolio. This is why ETFs are so helpful. They are not individual as they include dozens of instruments in one location.

Cryptocurrencies

This is a newer form of a financial instrument and one that is quickly growing. They are similar to currencies but are often called coins. Further, there are a variety of coins. One of the newer cryptocurrencies that is about to make an appearance is known as Libra. This is Facebook's upcoming coin that is meant to be global. Other coins that are currently popular and can be traded on the market are Bitcoin and Ethereum. Many experienced traders say beginners should not start with cryptocurrencies because of the high risk they have. The main reasons for this are because they can be easily hacked and often receive negative press.

Currencies

Currencies are a different type of financial instrument because they have to be traded in pairs. They are bought and sold in the forex market and are typically matched a certain way. For example, you will pair the American dollar with the Euro or the Canadian dollar with the Euro. Like cryptocurrencies, experienced traders stated that beginners should not start out with currencies. They can be tougher to understand and carry a larger risk than stocks. However, they are easier to trade than cryptocurrencies.

Options

When you use options to trade, you come to an agreement with another party. This agreement tells you when the financial instrument can be bought and sold. In order to take part in options trading, you need to have these requirements.

1. You need to include an expiration date in your agreement.

2. You can walk away from your agreement at any time.

3. You need to follow the process of the strike price, which is when the owner of the

financial instrument agrees to the price you set.

4. You need all the basic information on your financial instrument. This means that you don't decide on a company to trade in without doing your research and analyzing any charts.

Futures

Experienced traders feel that futures exchanges are the best way to get yourself started in the market. Like options, futures are an agreement of when a stock can be bought and sold. Sometimes there is no expiration date with futures; however, people typically include this because the stock cannot be traded until the agreed-upon price is reached. For instance, if the two parties state the stock will be traded once it reaches $450, then nothing can happen until the stock hits this price. This means you have no real idea when you will be able to buy or sell that stock.

One benefit of futures exchanges is that you are able to get real-time training in the stock market without having to spend too much time on various stocks. Instead, you can get an idea of how to analyze charts, research the history of companies you are interested in, and simply observe how the market runs. The whole time, you are still trading in the market because you have already set up an agreement.

Swing Futures Trading Tips For Beginners

There are dozens of tips that beginners can use to give them the best trading experience from the start. Here are some of the most popular tips to remember.

Research and Learn Every day

Before you start researching, it is essential that you read everything you can about swing trading. You will want to completely understand what swing trading is, it's benefits, risks, the best stocks to trade, and everything else involved in the process. Take your time researching to ensure you understand everything you are reading. Keep thorough notes and make sure they are close to you when you start trading. As you continue to learn, write down any valuable information in your notebook.

When it comes to your daily research, you will want to pay close attention to the historical charts for the stocks you are interested in. You will analyze the daily and weekly charts, so you can put together your trading plan for that stock. This plan will tell you when the best time to purchase the stock will be, depending on the stock's trends. You will also write down the best time to sell and your escape plan. An escape plan is when you set the lowest price you will hold the stock at. Once it reaches this price, you will sell the stock immediately. It doesn't matter if you haven't reached the highest point you thought the stock would reach during your analysis. In order to keep yourself from a greater capital loss, you follow your plan to sell the stock.

Treat Swing Trading Like a Career

Whether you are swing trading full or part-time, you want to treat it like you would any other job. You want to take it seriously. This means you will set up your schedule, limit distractions, and strengthen your self-discipline. You will want to follow all the rules and guidelines, including the ones you establish yourself, to the best of your abilities. Once you are able to do this, you are ready for a successful swing trading career.

Keep Your Emotions Out of Your Trades

One of the biggest steps you want to take when you start trading is to keep your emotions in check. If you need to find strategies that will allow you to control your emotions, such as meditation or deep breathing, you will want to practice these daily. You never want to make a trade because you let your emotions take control. When this happens, you are more likely to make a mistake which can cause you a lot of money.

Set Your Daily Schedule

Note the times of the stock market and make sure you are sitting in front of your computer during those times. This means you will want to start your day at least an hour before the stock market opens. You need to allow yourself time to read up on any news and get an idea of where your stocks and the stock market sits. The busiest time for trading is between 9:30 to around 11:00 A.M. and 2:00 to 3:30 P.M. Eastern time. However, you want to be cautious of making any trades before 10:00 A.M. Eastern time. This is because people are often trading their stocks between 9:30 and 10:00 A.M. because of the news they read about the stock's company. The first half-hour is a very chaotic time for the stock market, which can be very confusing for beginners. Therefore, it is best to wait to make any trades until the stock market has started to calm down but is still busy. Usually between 11:00 A.M. and 2:00 P.M. Eastern time is when people are taking lunch or spending their time researching and learning.

Once the stock market closes, you will want to take time to save any charts from the stocks you bought and sold. You will also want to make notes about your day in your journal. The notes you make can include how you were feeling and what your environmental conditions were as you purchased or traded a stock.

Don't Forget About Continuing Your Education

Sometimes one of the best ways to research is through educational courses that are available through swing trading websites. For example, "Guide to Stock Trading with Candlestick and Technical Analysis" is an online class that will help you learn how to analyze candlestick charts with technical analysis. This course is created for beginners and is only about $60 to take. There are other courses for both beginners and expert swing traders that you can consider taking as a part of your trading day.

Join an Online Community

Other than a broker, you will want to find someone who can help you learn the processes of swing trading. There are dozens of online communities such as The Trading Heroes Blog and Elite Swing Trading. Once you sign up for an account—sometimes you do have to pay—you will be able to connect with thousands of traders that will be happy to answer your questions or help you achieve your next step. Many of these community forums also keep everyone up-to-date on the news that can affect your stocks.

Keep Yourself in the Right Mindset

To reach your dreams of becoming a successful swing trader, you need to stay focused and stay in the right mindset. The basis of this mindset is having confidence in your abilities as a swing trader. You want to imagine yourself reaching your goals, whether this is building toward your retirement account or living comfortably as a swing trader.

Another part of this mindset is to have patience. It will take time to learn the stock market and be able to live off of your trades. Moreover, you need to have patience when it comes to the right moment. You don't want to purchase the stock or sell it before the exact moment in your trading plan.

By remaining flexible, you will be able to keep yourself in the right mindset. You want to understand that not everything is in your control. Focus on what is in your control, such as your actions. If something isn't in your control, accept it and move on.

You also want to keep your expectations realistic. Swing trading is not a career that will make you rich overnight. It will take time and energy to reach your desired success.

Mistakes Are Going to Happen

Part of being realistic is knowing that you will make mistakes. It doesn't matter how many years of experience you have as a swing trader, mistakes are going to happen. You can spend two weeks analyzing the charts for a promising stock, buy the stock, and then lose some of your capital because of a small mistake you made. Sometimes this happens because the stock market is unpredictable and no matter how well you research, you can't predict the future. When you do realize you made a mistake, learn from it and move on. If you worry about your past mistakes, you are going to affect your future trades. You will find yourself lacking the self-confidence you need to stay successful. Don't allow your mindset to decline because of a mistake.

Chapter 2   How Swing Trading Works?

What Swing Trading

Swing trading is a type of forex trading that endeavors to profit on a stock or any budgetary instrument over a time of a couple of days to half a month. Swing brokers fundamentally utilize specialized investigation to search for foreign currency trading openings. These merchants may use basic investigation notwithstanding examining value patterns and examples.

Swing trading is a short term trading style that involves you taking a position in the financial markets and staying with it for a number of days, perhaps weeks.

Swing trading is different from other types of trading such as position trading, day trading, high frequency trading or scalping mainly because of the period of time that a trade is held.

On one hand, some trading styles such as position trading allow you to take a position and then hold it for a longer period of time such as a couple of months or even years. On the other hand, a style such as scalping can involve holding a position for a few minutes, perhaps even seconds.

Therefore, a good way to think about swing trading is, a style that strikes a balance between both sides, offering more flexibility.

As a swing trader, you are mainly looking to profit from short term price changes or what is known as price swings in the markets. These opportunities are typically determined by technical analysis.

Swing trading vs. Day trading

Day trading is a completely different trading style. And the difference between the two comes down to the length of time that positions are held.

Day trading is a trading style in which you execute a number of positions in a day, but at the end of the day, you close all of them out. So, you may open a number of trades, say 10 of them in a day, but at the end of the day, you are flat.

Swing trading is regarded as more of a part time activity. In swing trading, you will be typically looking at longer time frames such as 3 hours, 4 hours, daily or weekly to spot swing trading opportunities. Therefore, this type of trading can be adopted by people who are or already employed in a different job. Day traders have the distinct advantage to take note of the price volatility that might be seen during a trading day. The volatility of prices on a daily basis is generally affected by big sellers or big buyers and has relatively less to do with the fundamentals of the company.

On the other hand, even though swing traders also use the help of technical indicators, the fundamental factors affecting the price of the security plays a very important role in the decision process for a swing trader. Swing traders look at particular chart patterns and use confirmation signals given by certain indicators to understand whether or not to enter or exit a particular trade. Swing traders as compared to day traders are not interested in the volatility in a stock price but are more bothered in understanding the underlying trend or the overall trend of the security.

Swing exchanging and day exchanging may appear comparative practices, however the real contrasts between the two have a typical topic: time.

Swing trading allows you take a more laid back approach. You can place a trade and walk away from your computer and not have to worry about it until may be the next day. So if your goal is to seek a source of income that is more passive, then swing trading is the way to go. It is also good for you if you are a person of mild temperament who doesn't like lots of action.

Truth be told, none of these trading styles is better than the other. It is just a matter of picking the trading style that fits you as a person and your current situation in life. You may want to consider the following before you make a decision:

- The amount of time that you can set aside for trading: If you are a busy person, you may want to consider swing trading.
- The amount of money that you have: Day trading may require that you start out with a lot of money since you will end up being dependent on it for your means of livelihood.

- Your personality: If you are more of a person who likes to take things nice and slow, you may want to stay away from day trading and opt for swing trading instead.
- Risk tolerance: Day trading is for you if you can withstand watching several trades going against you and still maintain your calmness. Swing trading is better if you are more of the calculating type who can only stand taking a loss once in a while.

Difference Between Swing Trading and Day Trading

The first question that you may have is how swing trading and day trading are different from each other. They both try and go after some of the trends that are going on in the market, and they are both short-term trades that you can work with.

The biggest difference that you will find with day trading and swing trading is how long you will hold your position. With day trading, you will purchase and sell the stock all on the same day before the market closes. With swing trading, you need to hold onto the stock at least overnight, if not up to a few weeks, depending on how the trend is going and how much you would like to make.

This can add in a little more risk and unpredictability to your trade. It is hard to know what gaps or up and down movements will happen in your position overnight, which is why most swing traders will be done using smaller position sizes than they would with day trading.

You get some choice in how long you would like to hold onto your position, which can reduce the risk a little bit. But it is always a good idea to have an idea of how long you will stay in the market ahead of joining.

As a swing trader, you will be responsible for looking at chart patterns over many days. Some of the most common patterns that you will find include triangles, flags, head and shoulders patterns, cup and handle patterns, and even moving average crossovers. You can also find reversal candlesticks, like hammers and shooting stars will help you to figure out the best time to join the market and make the biggest profit possible.

Swing trading has more risk than some of the longer - term options that you may choose to go with. With the long-term investments, you will find that you have the time and the relaxation to not worry about the big ups and downs in the market as much. Your account will end up evening out if you stay on the market long enough.

But with swing trading, this is not always going to work. You are only going to be in the market for up to a few weeks at the most. This means that if a trend does not go your way, you will lose out on money. You must do your research diligently before starting and make sure that you can accurately read the market. You only get a few weeks, which is more than what a day trader will get to work with, but adds in more risk, especially when you are working in an overnight position.

You have the choice of many investments, but if you would like to earn a lot of money within a week or less, then swing trading may be the option that you are looking for. Let's take a look at some of the strategies that you can use when it comes to swinging trading to ensure you are getting the best results possible.

Swing traders need to always remember that the opening of a stock might actually be remarkably different from how it closed the previous day. Swing traders often encounter issues with the wide spread between the ask and bid and the commissions which could take a great portion of their profits, however, this problem is much serious for day traders.

Also, unlike day traders that experience serious time commitment when trading since they need to pay attention to all open positions, swing traders may have few transactions in some days while they may not trade at all on other days. When you're a swing trader, you can check your positions periodically or they can be attended to with alerts especially when the price hits critical points. This is much better than monitoring the market constantly which could lead to apprehension and emotional trading.

Swing Trading vs. Position Trading

There is another type of stock trader who is commonly referred to as a position trader. Position traders are usually large institutions such as mutual funds, but individuals can be position traders as well. Position traders make investments in a company's stock for the long run. They may feel that a particular company or sector is undervalued and they are willing to take a position in the hope that eventually things will turn around and the market will value their company in line with where they see it going in the future.

Warren Buffett would be a good example of a position trader. He invests for the long term and takes positions in companies he considers to be undervalued, either because of market conditions or because he expects the companies' fundamentals to improve in the future.

Market Participants: Retail vs. Institutional Traders

More and more people are striking out on their own and doing their own self-directed investing. The Internet, with its plethora of information and tools, has primarily driven this trend, along with the opportunity to trade online without the use of a professional broker. Many investors have discovered that with a little work they can match or better the performance of many of the mutual fund managers, especially when taking into account the at times exorbitant management fees being charged by these money managers.

Individual Retail traders do have some advantages over Institutional traders. These Institutional traders are motivated to trade often and in large volumes. In comparison, Retail traders can wait for a good setup and trade when they see a good risk to reward opportunity. Institutional traders also have large accounts and cannot move their money in and out of a position as readily as a Retail trader. An Institutional trader is not going to take a 1,000 share position in the stock of a small company that trades 250,000 shares in a day. It is just too small for them to bother.

Ironically, large numbers of individual Retail traders will not use this advantage to their benefit and for various reasons they will instead overtrade. They succumb to greed and fear and that causes them to trade unwisely. Instead of being patient and exercising the self-discipline of winners, they become losers by overtrading. Retail traders who want to be successful in trading with the professionals must be patient. They must also recognize and manage the psychology of fear and greed and how it affects a trader's actions.

As a Retail trader, you can also play stocks that other Retail investors are playing. Checking in on social media sites like StockTwits and Twitter will give you a good sense of where Retail investors are investing their money, however, do not get caught up in the specifics of all of the posts. There are lots of twits on StockTwits making wild predictions and touting how they just made $7,000.00 on a trade in XYZ Company. Take everything you read with a large grain of salt.

Benefits of Swing Trading

Swing trading has less risk: When compared to working with day trading, you will find that swing trading has less risk. This is because you get more time to work in the market. It is often hard to estimate how a stock will do throughout a single day.
You can swing trade along with other trades
Many traders will choose to work on swing trading along with day trading all at the same time. During the market hours, they will focus most of their energy on their day trading position.
Overnight trading can be an advantage
Some traders believe that trading overnight will harm them. They are worried about some of the trends that could happen to their stock while they are asleep.
More time to look at the market
Day trading has to be done really quickly. You don't get a lot of time to watch the markets, and you may need to make split-second decisions to get results. With swing trading, you can analyze the market over time, and you have more time to make your trading decisions. This takes away some of the pressure of your trades, and it is easier to earn money in this manner without all the stress.

Potential to reach the trades better

Compared to working with day trading, you are more likely to reach the trades that you would like with swing trading. You will be able to watch the market, predict how the trades will do over a few days or a few weeks, rather than a few hours, and make more money.

More daily freedom

If you are a day trader, you have to spend all day watching your trades. Little changes up or down in the market will make a big difference in day trading, and this can be really stressful if you are getting started. Many of the people who decide to go with swing trading tried out day trading in the past but didn't like all the stress that went with it and didn't like having to stare at their computer screens all day long. Swing trading can provide you with a similar profit without all the hassle.

Generating consistent income

Long term investors are more bothered with wealth creation or wealth preservation. They are not bothered about generating consistent monthly income. On the other hand successful swing traders can easily generate consistent income for themselves on a monthly basis.

Holding different securities to diversify your risk
High-Frequency Trades
There are a number of investment banks, funds and other companies that base their trading on sophisticated computer algorithms. They trade frequently and at lightning speed. To illustrate how important speed is to these firms, some have located close to the exchanges while others install dedicated fiber optic cables to gain a tiny fraction of a microsecond execution on a trade. These types of trades are referred to as High-Frequency Trades (HFT) due to how often they happen during a normal trading day.

How to Start Trading

Choosing to Buy Long or Sell Short

When you are setting up an account to trade, you will probably need to take the time to fill out some additional forms with the broker so that you can take this short position with a stock. You should also have an idea that this option can be riskier compared to just going long or purchasing a stock, so you must be actively there to manage the position.

When the stock starts to move down, shareholders are going to fear that they will have to lose their profits or gains, and they move to sell that quickly. This selling activity is going to feed into more selling as shareholders continue to take the profits and traders start to shorten. This additional shorting activity adds to the downward pressure that is there on the price. This sends the price of the stock into a strong decline, which means that short sellers are able to make a good amount of profits while long traders and other investors are going to enter panic mode and may try to dump their shares to protect themselves.

As a swing trader, when you are ready to enter into a position, you are going to have two choices. You can either go in or pay the price that the seller is asking for right away or you can place a bid that is at or below the bid price. Paying the asking price immediately can be beneficial because it ensures that the purchase transaction is completed or filled but may mean that you will pay more for it.

Picking out a Broker

During this process, we also need to take some time to discuss picking out a broker. If you have already gotten into other forms of trading in the past, then you can simply work with the same broker that you already have. But, if you are getting into trading and this is the first one you have done before, then you will need to search to find the right broker for you. There are many different brokers out there, and many of them can assist you with swing trading. The biggest thing that you will want to look at is the commissions and fees that each broker assesses against you. Since swing trading times are relatively short and you will enter into and out of trades within a few weeks at most with each trade, you want to make sure that the profits you make aren't eaten up by the commissions to your broker.

There are different methods that the broker can use to come up with their fees. Some will charge a fixed rate for the whole year. This often works well for long-term trades and probably won't be an option available to you since you will do more trades. The two options that you will most likely deal with include a fee for each trade or a fee based on how much profit you earn.

Before you enter into any trade, make sure that you discuss the fees with your broker. They should be able to outline their fees and can discuss with you where your money will go when you work with them. This can help you to get a good idea of how much you will spend based on how much you earn, how many trades you decide to enter into, and more. Get the commissions and fees in writing, along with any other agreements that you and the broker and their firm agree to in order to protect you.

Make sure that your broker is regulated by the government. This is the first and most important aspect that you should always look for before anything. Never skip this one.

Ensure that they have quality customer service. Nobody deserves your money or your business if they have poor customer service; at least not in this competitive world.

Bad customer service is a symptom of a much worse problem. If they can't take care of how they handle you as a client, how are they supposed to do better when it comes to your money? You are much better shopping around for someone else who is more competent.

Trading is a tough business in which the risk of losing your money very fast is real. Therefore, managing risk is of utmost importance. If your broker is charging you heavy commissions on your trades, this raises your risk and you will likely be out of business in no time.

Website and account security. In this day and age of web hackers, your broker has to invest heavily in their security. Matters dealing with finance cannot be left to chance, and your broker has to show that they respect this. Remember, you will be trusting your broker to process financial transactions using your debit or credit card, among other things.

Quality trading tools. A high quality trading platform that packages all high quality indicators can really make for a smooth experience in trading.

Picking out How Much You Want to Invest

It is best to start out by putting in an amount that you are comfortable losing. No one hopes to lose money on any of their trades. But, it does happen, especially when you are a beginner. Putting in just the amount that you would be willing to lose if something goes wrong can help to reduce the amount of risk that you are taking on.

Getting started with swing trading can be exciting. This is a fun type of trading that moves quickly and can help you to earn a good profit in a short amount of time but still doesn't require you to spend all day on the computer watching how the trade is going.

Buying Long or Selling Short

As a trader, you need to learn more about long and short buying and selling. Trades usually commence via purchase first or selling first. To define the terms appropriately, we need to learn about the meaning and implication of each.

Long position: When you assume a long position on a stock, the implication here is that you own the security and it belongs to you. There is no debt on it. Therefore, when a trader buys an asset, he has taken a long position on the asset. In this instance, he hopes that the asset price will appreciate so that he can sell it at a higher price.

Short position: We also have a short position where a trader actually sells stocks that he or she does not own. These are stocks or financial instruments that belong to another. Selling short simply means selling in the hope of making money from the sale in order to repay the owner and make a profit in the process. Short sales occur when a trader is trading the markets, sees an opportunity but lacks the funds or means to execute the trade. Many experienced traders come across opportunities they believe are profitable. In such instances, they get into an agreement with their broker to access stocks they do not own.

Day traders are often associated with short sales. They often sell stocks then purchase them hoping to benefit from the price difference. They sell stocks that they do not own at a high price and then buy back the same stocks when the price falls. While this can be profitable, it is a risky venture that should only be practiced by seasoned traders.

Short sales by traders are often settled by delivery of the "borrowed" security back to the real owner. Most stocks that are sold short often belong to investors but are held by brokers. As a trader, if you wish to short sell, then you first need to identify an opportunity in the market. You will then need to access the stock so that you can sell it without owning it. This is of course after your market analysis shows some profit potential.

Others who also engage in short selling are market makers. Market makers are also known as liquidity providers. They do this in order to mitigate the risk of a long position on the same stock or in response to unexpected demand. Market makers hope to benefit financially from a bid-offer spread.

Traders who engage in short selling can borrow stocks from brokerage firms. Brokerage firms often have an inventory of stocks lying around. Some of these belong to the brokerage while others belong to other long-term investors. It is important to note that even as you gain access to stocks that you do now own, there are certain rules and conditions attached. These include fees and other charges as well as rules. For instance, you can expect to be charged a certain fee for the privilege. You will also be required to pay any dividend due to the stock's owner while the stocks are under your control.

Short selling is an important tool for a swing trader because stock prices usually drop much more quickly than they go up. It is a commonly held rule of thumb that stocks fall 3 times faster than they rise.

Shorting stocks as a legitimate trading activity is still hotly debated today. Some feel that short sellers unnecessarily punish investors by causing stocks to drop faster and in larger moves than otherwise would have occurred. In addition, short sellers can use social media and other methods to spread inaccurate information to cause a stock price to drop.

In order to start short selling, you will open a margin account through your broker. This account will use your profits in your account as collateral, just as a car is used as collateral for a vehicle loan. This means that if you are unable to repay your broker back in any way, your broker still receives the money as he or she can take it right out of your account.

The biggest risk is that you can never really tell the future. No matter how much you analyze charts or the general stock market conditions, such as if it's a bull or bear market, you will never be able to officially tell what a stock or the market is going to do.

While short selling occurs in a way that is meant to protect the trader's account, you also want to make sure that you understand that you can still bring yourself into debt if the process doesn't work as well as it should. You will also want to make sure that you go through the same trading plan, research, and following all your rules and guidelines before you decide to short sell.

How to Enter a Trade?

These spreads in the bid and ask can vary for each stock and even for the same stock at different times of the day. If the stock does not have a lot of buyers and sellers, then the spread could be quite large (up to $0.50 or more per share). If there are lots of buyers and sellers, then the spread between the bid and ask could be as low as $0.01 per share.

When a swing trader wants to enter a position, they have 2 choices. They can pay what the seller is asking immediately or they can place a bid at or below the current bid price. Paying the ask immediately ensures that the order is filled (filled means the purchase transaction is completed). When a trader places a bid at or below the current bid price, they may get a purchase at a lower price. The disadvantage of this purchase option is that the trader may not get their order filled. For example, if a trader puts in a bid to buy an uptrending stock, the bid may never get filled, leaving the trader without an entry in a profitable trade.

Investment and Margin Accounts

Investing on margin means that you are borrowing funds, in order to make deals. This also is called leveraging. Investments may be leveraged at a given ratio. For example, if the leverage on an investment is 2:1, it means that, for every physical dollar on the deal, there are two which are debt.

Investing on margin can be an amazing, tool as it acts as a multiplier. However, this strategy can backfire when the price of the asset does not go up, and the investor gets a "margin call", that is, they have to pay up. If the investor does not have the money to pay up, then they may be deemed as insolvent. This may lead the investor to be kicked out. In the case of large financial institutions, insolvency is a huge deal and may lead to the bankruptcy of entire financial institutions.

So, the moral of the story is to always have enough cash or highly-liquid assets, such as bonds, which can be liquidated fairly quickly in the case of a margin call.

Margin Trading Account

The margin trading account keeps a line of credit to your firm with helping you buy the stocks through the brokerage firm which also keeps the securities under consideration if you want to. There are numerous options to open the account with the margin accounts. You can opt out the possibility of buying the right purchase without listing out any price of a specific stock in the market. You have to consider, and without any complications, you will have the account with you to get into the stock market.

Understanding Margin

When you get the margin, it means that the brokerage offers your o have the trading account. You have to remember that the purchase of the credit is needed with the new stocks in there. In this case, you borrow the money from someone to have the investors over the trades. It also saves the interested when you are holding the position with keeping it overnight with the interest rate which is over the course. You have to follow the dependency over the time with the slight usage of 2% and how it helps in improving the right side of the margin with allowing it to be the right profit for you which you could use for putting it in the market with the market all along.

Requirements to open an account

There are some of the policies and procedures which everyone has to follow when it comes to opening the trading account. You have to provide the information and also help yourself to get familiar with it as soon as you can. The rule of the brokerage firms inquires your personal information such as your name, address, email address, SSN, date of birth, place of employment, tax bracket and much more. You may be hesitant at first with giving out such information, but that is required for you to fulfill the policies to get the trading account on your name. They require you to show the history of your work experience in some cases when there is a need for an inquiry. There are many questions which you have to, so you have to be patient through the process. It is always about the right move which you make to understand what the deal is going on another side. There are many other things which the brokerage firms will be asking from you, so you have to keep the items clear and be answerable to them. It will be about the registration and how you developed the interest in getting the account.

Chapter 3   Platforms And Tools For Trading

To be a successful trader, you will need access to reliable resources. The good news is that there are plenty of excellent resources all across the web. These resources include educational materials, online brokers, real-time securities markets data, and super-fast computer networks.

Sometimes you may not have access to all the resources necessary and you may have to choose between what is essential and what you can afford. A little research goes a long way in helping you make crucial decisions about your trades. It is advisable to know more about the kind of resources available to you. These resources are ideal for swing traders.

Swing Trading Tools

Traders are always searching for the best trading systems and ways they can develop these systems to suit their trading styles. Fortunately, there is a process that any trader can use in order to discover their preferred trading mode and system.

Identifying Best Strategies for Profitability

There are plenty of small but crucial things you can do as a swing trader to improve your success. For instance, you could begin by identifying the location of the swing low and swing high positions on a particular chart. If you are able to note the swings accurately, then you will be able to place accurate trades which will increase your profitability greatly.

Swing Highs and Swing Lows

Swing highs and swing lows are also referred to as SHSL. This refers to the price action where multiple bars and candlesticks are joined together so that they are viewed as a single move in a given direction. The movement is generally known as a leg. Sometimes it is also known as swing or a move. This is where the term swing originates from.

The swing represents a single part of the price action in a particular direction. This swing is always closely countered by a swing in the opposite direction. Sometimes this movement is sideways rather than back and forth. As it is, price moves back and forth in the market. In other words, it swings back and forth and hence the term swing. The highest point of a swing is the swing high while the lowest point is known as the swing low.

How to Identify Swings

The market is constantly in motion. A swing occurs when there are two consecutive lower highs and lower lows or when there are two consecutive higher lows and higher highs. Remember that swings appear in all manner of shapes and sizes. However, the rule on how to identify them is very simple. Simply look for consecutive higher highs and higher lows or consecutive lower highs and lower lows.

Swings are bullish if the general movement is upwards and bearish if the general movement is downwards. Sometimes a new low will appear when the trend is upwards. At other times a new high will appear when the general trend is headed downwards. When this happens, you should not be worried or concerned as these are considered false swings. Unless there are consecutive highs or lows, then ignore everything else.

Use Swings to Increase Profitability

We have learned how to identify swings in the market. Now we need to apply this knowledge in order to be profitable. The first step is to place your stop-loss points. This should be slightly above the higher high for a bearish situation and below the lowest low in a bullish situation.

Also, the correct and accurate swing highs and swing lows provide an opportunity to draw Fibonacci extensions. These lines will enable you to identify target areas of high probability. As such, it becomes possible to place our take profit and stop-loss points on our charts. Remember Livermore? The gentleman said to be one of the most successful traders ever? Back in 19 29, he managed to make about $100 million. In today's terms, this is equivalent to almost $1.4 billion. That is a lot of money even for an experienced trader.

If you learn about the best trading systems, then you too can make plenty of money in today's prevailing marketing rates. You could always trade with the market trend or against it. Remember that it is always advisable to follow the trend rather than the opposite. Only oppose the trend if you are an experienced swing trader and know exactly what you are doing. Key will be identifying the best entry points into a trade and the best places to collect profits as well as exit trades.

Before you begin your swing, trading ventures, ensure that you come up with a tested plan that you can implement. Therefore, test your preferred systems and strategies and ensure that they are working as desired. This way, you will be able to prepare appropriately and trade successfully and profitably over time.

Swing traders are always searching for conditions in the markets where stock prices are looking to swing either downwards or possibly upwards. There are numerous technical indicators that are available to enhance your trades. Indicators used in swing trading are basically essential in identifying trends in the market between certain trading periods.

These trading periods that range anywhere from 3 to 15 are then analyzed using our technical indicators in order to determine the presence or otherwise of resistance and support levels. If these have actually materialized and are clearly visible, then we can proceed to make other determinations.

At this stage, you will also need to determine whether any trend is bullish or bearish. You will also need to be on the lookout for a reversal because without one you will not be able to enter a trade. Reversals are also referred to as countertrends or pullbacks. As soon as we can clearly point out the reversal, then we can easily identify the appropriate entry point.

The entry point should be the point where the pullback is just about to come to an end and the trend is about to pick up again. Being able to determine these points is really crucial. This same approach is the very same one used by Jesse Livermore to earn his wealth.

Benefits

Swing trading offers some of the best risks to reward opportunities compared to other trading strategies. This means that for a smaller amount, you will stand to win a much larger profit. Trading is a risky venture but swing trading has a better payoff compared to others. As such, you stand to make more money at reduced risks compared to traders using different trading styles like day traders or position traders.

Another benefit is that a lot of intraday noise will be eliminated using this approach. Smart money traders are always on the lookout for big swings and this is what you will also be doing. This approach is less stressful and potentially more profitable compared to other strategies.

You will also have a lot of time in your hands compared to other traders. Day traders and others often spend hours each day glued to their screens. Their days are not just spent staring at the screen but their stress levels are extremely high. Constant stress will result in fast burn-out and emotional trading which are not good for long-term successful trading.

Best Indicators for Swing Traders

There are plenty of indicators that traders and investors use to enhance their trades. We shall review just a few of these and discover the best way of applying them to our trades in order to maximize profitability. It is crucial to understand that none of these indicators will make you profitable from the onset. Therefore, do not break your back trying to find the best or most profitable trade indicators. Instead, focus more on learning about a couple of extremely effective indicators as well as the strategies and methods used alongside them. Experts believe that trading strategies are more profitable when you apply the few indicators that you have mastered.

1. Moving Averages

Moving averages are among the most important trade indicators used by swing traders. They are defined as lines drawn across a chart and are determined based on previous prices. Moving averages are really simple to understand yet they are absolutely useful when it comes to trading the markets. They are extremely useful to all kinds of traders include swing traders, day, intra, and long-term investors.

You need to ensure that you have a number of moving averages plotted across your trading charts all with different time periods. For instance, you can have the 100-day moving average, the 50-day, and the 9-day MA. This way, you will obtain a much broader overview of the market and be able to identify much stronger reversals and trends.

How to use Moving Averages

Once you have plotted and drawn the moving averages on your charts, you can then use them for a number of purposes. The first is to identify the strength of a trend. Basically, what you need to do is to observe the lines and gauge their distance from the current stock price.

A trend is considered weak if the trend and the current price are far from the relative MA. The farther they are then the weaker the trend is. This makes it easier for traders to note any possible reversals and also identify exit and entry points. You should move averages together with additional indicators, for instance, the volume.

Moving averages can also be used to identify trend reversals. When you plot multiple moving averages, they are bound to cross. If they do, then this implies a couple of things. For instance, crossing MA lines indicate a trend reversal. If these cross after an uptrend, then it means that the trend is about to change direction and a bearish one is about to appear. However, some trend reversals are never real so you have to be careful before calling out one. Many traders are often caught off guard by these false reversals. Therefore, confirm them before trading using other tools and methods. Even then, the moving average is a very vital indicator. They enable traders to get a true feel and understanding of the markets.

2. RSI – Relative Strength Index

Another crucial indicator that is commonly used by swing traders and other traders are the RSI or relative strength index. This index is also an indicator that evaluates the strength of the price of a security that you may be interested in. The figure indicated is relative and provides traders with a picture of how the stock is performing relative to the markets. You will need information regarding volatility and past performance. All traders, regardless of their trading styles, need this useful indicator. Using this relative evaluation tool gives you a figure that lies between 1 and 100.

Tips on RSI Use

The relative strength index is ideally used for identifying divergence. Divergence is used by traders to note trend reversals. We can say that divergence is a disagreement or difference between two points. There are bearish and bullish divergent signals. Very large and fast movements in the markets sometimes produce false signals. This is why it advisable to always use indicators together with other tools.

You can also use the RSI to identify oversold and overbought conditions. It is crucial that you are able to identify these conditions as you trade because you will easily identify corrections and reversals. Sometimes securities are overbought at the markets when this situation occurs, it means that there is a possible trend reversal and usually the emerging trend is bearish. This is often a market correction. Basically, when a security is oversold, it signals a correction or bullish trend reversal but when it's overbought, it introduces a bearish trend reversal.

The theory aspect of this condition requires a ratio of 70:30. This translates to 70% overvalued or over purchased and 30% undervalued or oversold. However, in some cases, you might be safer going with an 80/20 ratio just to prevent false breakouts.

3. Volume

When trading, the volume is a crucial indicator and constitutes a major part of any trading strategy. As a trader, you want to always target stocks with high volumes as these are considered liquid. How many traders, especially new ones, often disregard volume and look at other indicators instead.

While volume is great for liquidity purposes, it is also desirable for trend. A good trend should be supported by volume. A large part of any stock's volume should constitute part of any trend for it to be a true and reliable trend.

Most of the time traders will observe a trend based on price action. You need to also be on the lookout for new money which means additional players and volume. If you note significant volumes contributing to a trend, then you can be confident about your analysis. Even when it comes to a downtrend, there should be sufficient volumes visible for it to be considered trustworthy. A lack of volume simply means the stock has either been undervalued or overvalued.

4. Bollinger Bands Indicator

One of the most important indicators that you will need is the Bollinger band indicator. It is a technical indicator that performs two crucial purposes. The first is to identify sections of the market that are overbought and oversold. The other purpose is to check the market's volatility.

This indicator consists of 3 distinct moving averages. There is a central one which is an SMA or simple moving average and then there two on each side of the SMA. These are also moving averages but are plotted on either side of the central SMA about 2 standard deviations away.

Accumulation and Distribution Line

Another indicator that is widely used by swing traders is the accumulation/distribution line. This indicator is generally used to track the money flow within security. The money that flows into and out of stock provides useful information for your analysis.

The accumulation/distribution indicator compares very well with another indicator, the OBV, or the on-balance volume indicator. The difference, in this case, is that it considers the trading range as well as the closing price of a stock. The OBV only considers the trading range for a given period.

When the security closes out close to its high, then the accumulation/distribution indicator will add weight to the stock value compared to closing out close to the mid-point. Depending on your needs and sometimes the calculations, you may want to also use the OBV indicator.

You can use this indicator to confirm an upward trend. For instance, when it is trending upwards, you will observe buying interest because the security will close at a point that is higher than the mid-range. However, when it closes at a point that is lower than the mid-range, then the volume is indicated as negative and this indicates a declining trend.

While using this indicator, you will also want to be on the lookout for divergence. When the accumulation/distribution begins to decline while the price is going up, then you should be careful because this signals a possible reversal. On the other hand, if the trend starts to ascend while the price is falling, then this probably indicates a possible price rise in the near future. It is advisable to ensure that your internet and other connections are extremely fast especially when using these indicators as time is of the essence.

The Average Directional Index, ADX

Another tool or indicator that is widely used by swing traders is the average directional index, the ADX. This indicator is basically a trend indicator and its purpose is largely to check the momentum and strength of a trend. A trend is believed to have directional strength if the ADX value is equal to or higher than 40. The directional could be upward or downward based on the general price direction. However, when the ADX value is below 20, then we can say that there is no trend or there is one but it is weak and unreliable.

You will notice the ADX line on your charts as it is mainline and is often black in color. There are other lines that can be shown additionally. These lines are DI- and DI+ and in most cases are green and red in color respectively. You can use all the three lines to track both the momentum and the trend direction.

Aroon Technical Indicator

Another useful indicator that you can use is the Aroon indicator. This is a technical indicator designed to check if financial security is trending. It also checks to find out whether the security's price is achieving new lows or new highs over a given period of time.

You can also use this technical indicator to discover the onset of a new trend. It features two distinct lines which are the Aroon down line and the Aroon up line. A trend is noted when the Aaron up line traverses across the Aaron down line. To confirm the trend, then the Aaron up line will get to the 100-point mark and stay there.

The reverse holds water as well. When the Aroon down line cuts below the Aaron up line, then we can presume a downward trend. To confirm this, we should note the line getting close to the 100-point mark and staying there.

This popular trading tool comes with a calculator which you can use to determine the number of things. If the trend is bullish or bearish, then the calculator will let you know. The formulas used to determine this refer to the most recent highs and lows. When the Aroon values are high, then recent values were used and when they are low, the values used were less recent. Typical Aroon values vary between o and 100. Figures that are close to 0 indicate a weak trend while those closer to 100 indicate a strong trend.

The bullish and bearish Aroon indicators can be converted into one oscillator. This is done by making the bearish one range from 0 to -100 while the bullish one ranges from 100 to 0. The combined indicator will then oscillate between 100 and -100. 100 will indicate a strong trend, 0 means there is no trend while -100 implies a negative or downward trend.

This trading tool is pretty easy to use. What you need to is first obtain the necessary figures then plot these on the relevant chart. When you then plot these figures on the chart, watch out for the two key levels. These are 30 and 70. Anything above the 70-point mark means the trend is solid while anything below 30 implies a weak trend.

Trading Platforms

Trading platforms are the actual platforms or software programs that enable traders to place their trades and monitor their accounts. An electronic trading platform is a computer program of a website with a user interface where traders place financial trades.

As a swing trader, you will use this platform to enter, close, exit, and manage positions. This is often done via an intermediary such as your broker. Most traders use online platforms which are overseen and offered by brokerage firms. Brokers charge a fee when you use their platforms but sometimes, they offer discounts to traders who make a certain number of trades each month or those with funded accounts.

Basic Swing Trading Platforms

Trading platforms provide traders with the opportunity to place trades and monitor their accounts. There is a variety of platforms available to swing traders. They come with a number of different features. These include premium research functions, a news feed, charting tools, and even real-time price quotes. These additional features and tools enhance a trader's performance and make it easier to execute trades faster and accurately. Most platforms available today are designed for different financial instruments like Forex, stocks, futures, and options.

We basically have two different types of platforms. These are commercial platforms and prop platforms. Commercial platforms are mostly used by traders such as swing traders, retail investors, and day traders. They are largely easy to use and come with a myriad of features such as charts and a news feed.

We also have prop platforms. These are platforms that are customized for specific users such as institutional investors and large brokerage firms. Apparently, their needs are much different compared to those of small traders and retail investors. The prop platforms are designed to take into consideration the different needs of these special clients.

As a swing trader, you will most likely be using commercial platforms provided by different brokerage firms. Even then, there are some things that you need to be on the lookout before choosing one. For instance, what are the included features? How about costs and fees charged? Also, different traders will require different tools on their platforms. There are certain tools that are suitable for day and swing traders while others are more suitable for options and futures traders.

When selecting a platform, always watch out for the fees charged. As a small-scale, retail swing trader, you want to trade on one that charges low and affordable fees. However, sometimes there are certain trade-offs. For instance, some platforms charge low fees but they lack certain crucial features or provide poor services. Others may seem expensive but provide crucial features including research tools and excellent services. So, you will need to consider all these factors before eventually selecting a suitable trading platform.

There is yet another crucial point to keep in mind when selecting a trading platform. Some platforms are available only through specific brokers or intermediaries. Other platforms are universal and work with different brokerage platforms and intermediaries across the board. Traders also select trading platforms based on their own personal styles and preferences.

You should find out if there are any particular requirements or conditions that require to be fulfilled. For instance, some platforms require traders to maintain at least $25,oo0 in their trading accounts in the form of equity and possibly cash as well. In this instance, a trader may then receive approval for credit which is also known as margin.

Examples of Swing Trading Platforms

1. The Home Trading System

The home trading system is an algorithm and trading software designed to improve performance. Using this system, you can expect to make smarter, faster and better trading decisions. This particular platform comes with innovative features and a custom algorithm that combines seamlessly to provide a real-time fully integrated trading platform. You are bound to benefit from this platform and experience the benefits of seamless trading complete with all the features that you need.

The platform is completely compatible with some of the most dynamic and highly reliable charting tool. It is able to work with all kinds of markets from stocks to Forex and indices. The platform is compatible with a variety of bars such as range and momentum bars as well as tick charts.

The designers of this platform took great care to consider all the different kinds of traders. This is why this specific platform is suitable for day traders, swing traders, Forex traders, retail investors, and long-term traders. The Home Trading System constitutes a modular platform that consists of different core features. A lot of these features can easily be switched off and on depending on the situation or to suit a particular requirement.

One of the advantages of this platform is that it endeavors to make trading extremely simple. For instance, the algorithm automatically colors the candlesticks or bars a red or blue color in order to provide a clear view of the market conditions and trends. The system will continue following the trends and mark any major changes in a contrasting color. For instance, whenever there is a trigger bar, these will appear in a different color so that it is clear to you the trader that there is definite variation in the trend.

This color feature not only makes trading easy but also improves your trading psychology so that you can trade with very little worry. Other desirable parameters that are essential to your trades are also provided on the platform. For instance, you need accurate and reliable trading signals delivered at the right time. Fortunately, the Home Trading System is designed to provide these signals in a timely and accurate manner.

When there is a turning point in the momentum of stock in the markets, then this will be detected and a change of color will clearly indicate the turning point. You will be able to see a blue color with contrasting orange color pointing out areas of interest. The dots will indicate the entry points, exit points, collect profit points and so on. A stop point is also indicated just in case the trade does not work out as planned and you need to exit.

2. The Entry Zone Platform

We also have a swing trading platform known as the Entry Zone. This platform has been around for a while but has recently undergone a complete overhaul. It has received a new design to specifically address the needs of swing traders. There is no trader in the entire world who wants to join an over-extended market even when it features a large stop-loss point.

One of the main benefits of this specific platform is that it helps eliminate the challenge of entering an overly extended market. It starts by first checking for a pullback. It does this by accessing the 60-minute timeframe. This way, you will be protected from accessing the markets at the worst moment. The algorithm is able to proceed and track the markets so that you eventually get to find out the best market entry points.

3. Able Trend Trading Platform

This is another platform designed with swing traders in mind. One of its most outstanding features is its ability to instantly identify changes in the trend. Trend direction is first indicated by a distinct color. When the signal is headed upwards then the color is blue and when it heads downwards it changes color to red. If there is any sideways movement then the color changes once more to green.

This platform, therefore, makes it pretty easy to observe the market trend and keep abreast with it. Additional information will then enable you to make the necessary trade moves that you need to as a swing trader. For instance, you will notice red and blue dots on your screen. These indicate the various stop points. When there is a downward trend, then the red dots will indicate your sell points while blue dots will indicate your buy points on the upward trend. These stop points ensure that you partake of the large market movements but with very little risk or exposure.

The reasons why this system is so successful is that it comes with state of the art features. It generates dot and bar colors that you can choose for the different bar charts. These include the 5-minute, 1-minute, daily, tick, and weekly charts. Many traders have termed this platform as both robust and functional. It is a universal platform that can work with different trading systems.

You are able to make large profits if you are able to enter the markets and join the trend at an early stage. Identifying the trend is easy when you have this software. Remember that the trend is a friend of any swing trader. Therefore, spend some time at the beginning of your trades to identify the trend and then move on from here. Identifying the trend at an early stage is what you wish to do. The risks to you are minimal at this stage. This platform helps you identify the trend and provide you with additional crucial information that even large investors do not have.

You are able to operate on any market so that you are not limited to trading stocks only. If you wish to swing trade options, currencies, and other instruments, then you are free to do so. The platform is suitable for all trading styles including day trading, swing trading, and position trading, and so on.

4. Interactive Brokers

This is a popular platform that has been recently revamped. It is highly rated software because of the useful tools available to traders. Some of these tools are extremely useful to sophisticated or seasoned traders who need more than just the basics.

This platform is able to connect you to any and all exchanges across the world. For instance, you may want to trade markets in Hong Kong, Australia, and so on. The software is able to seamlessly connect you so that you have great trading experience.

This platform has seen the addition of new features which make trading even easier. These are, however, more suitable to seasoned traders who are more sophisticated than the average retail investor or small trader.

One of the attractive features of Interactive Brokers is that it is a very affordable platform to use. It is especially cost-friendly to small scale traders, retail investors, and the ordinary swing trader as the margin rates are low and affordable.

The platform supports trading across 120 markets located in at least 31 countries and deals in more than 23 different currencies. It also supports traders who execute trades pretty fast.

Trading and Data

As a trader, you will be making most of your decisions based on data. You, therefore, need to have access to reliable data such as stock prices and so on. Long term investors do not necessarily worry about accurate stock prices in the short term. However, for swing traders, it is essential to have access to the latest trading data.

The good news is that most online brokers provide traders with some form of data. All this data is mostly free. The platforms consistently receive data streams throughout. This data is crucial for most traders. Sometimes real-time data is not free and as a trader, you will need to determine which data you need and which type you will pay for. Always ensure that you have access to all the data you require during trading.

Chapter 4   Financial Instruments for Swing Trading

One of the most difficult parts of swing trading, especially for a beginner, is finding the best market for you. This includes what type of financial instruments you want to focus on when it comes to trading. There are a variety of financial instruments; such as ETFs, futures, options, currencies, cryptocurrencies, and stocks. As a beginner, it is important to try to find one financial instrument that you are comfortable with.

Stocks

Stock are probably the most common financial instrument that people think of when they start their trading career. In fact, most people probably believe that this is the financial instrument they will be trading. Part of this is because of the popularity. However, another part is because they really don't realize how many financial instruments there are when it comes to trading.

When people talk about stocks in the trading community, they will often refer to them as shares. There are several ways you can handle shares. At the same time, you want to make sure that you are focusing on stocks that are within your target companies. For example, you might want to focus on blue-chip stocks. Therefore, if you find a stock that isn't considered blue-chip, you will want to move on. One of the biggest downsides to choosing stocks is that each stock you take on will carry its own individual risk. This means that no matter what type of negative news comes about the company for a stock you hold, such as Google or Twitter, you will have the risk of losing money due to the negative news. However, there is a way to trade stocks without having to think of each stock carrying it's own risk and this is through ETFs.

As a speculator or trader, you are not concerned with the financial stability of a company or its fundamental value of its stock because the way the activity works well, is if you look to profit in the short term, from the rising and falling of prices.

ETFs

ETFs are known as Exchange-Traded Funds. When you think of ETFs you can picture a bunch of stocks in one basket. What this group of stocks or other securities you decide to trade do is analyze the underlying index of the fund. There are a variety of ETFs. For example, you can choose an ETF that follows more of a target, such as retail companies or you could choose an ETF that has more variety within its basket. While you are looking at different ETFs, you want to keep in mind the same rules and guidelines for yourself that you do for stocks or any other type of financial instrument. While ETFs used to be focused more towards stocks, they can now focus on bonds, currencies, and even looking into cryptocurrencies.

One of the biggest pros to ETFs is you are able to have variety through purchasing one ETF because it is made up of different securities. Many people believe that this can save you money because if you decided to purchase the stocks in the ETF separately, you would be spending more money. For example, if you are interested in stocks that focus on space, you can look for an ETF that has this target instead of having to purchase a dozen or more separate stocks. In fact, most ETFs can hold hundreds of stocks.

Another positive of ETFs is you don't have to worry so much if one of the company's securities start to fall because of negative press as the other securities will help balance out the fall. Therefore, you might not even notice that price drop from one security. Because of this, many traders feel that ETFs are a good risk management instrument.

The price also tends to be more of a positive when it comes to ETFs. While most people believe that they will be expensive because they hold so many securities from different companies, this method of thinking isn't true. In fact, you might find that many ETFs are cheaper than some of the most popular blue-chip stocks on the market. On top of this, some ETFs might have a blue-chip stock within them.

Diversification is one of the terms that you will often run into as a trader. Diversification basically means that you have a variety of stock or whatever type of financial instrument you decide to trade. This is another reason why many traders look at ETFs as they will offer diversification through their variety of stocks. However, many traders and investors feel that diversification can also be a negative in the stock world. While it is highly debated, some people feel that if you have too much diversification in your account, then you can find yourself struggling to manage some risks.

Currencies

Trading currencies is just like trading money when you go on a vacation. For example, if you live in Canada and you decide to travel to Europe, you will have to trade your Canadian money in for Euros. In a sense, trading currencies in the stock market works the same way. You will always need to have two different currencies in order to trade. You will also want to watch to see what the value of the money is through a comparison. For example, some currencies receive a higher value compared to others while other currencies receive a lower value.

One important piece of advice from many experienced swing traders is that most of them agree that you should not start out trading using currencies as your financial instrument. They really believe that after you use simulation trading, you should turn your attention to stocks as these are often considered to be a base in the trading world. Stocks have been around an incredibly long time, which often helps beginners as they are learning the guidelines, rules, and how to trade in general.

Cryptocurrencies

A Cryptocurrency is a form of virtual or digital currency that can be used as medium of exchange, much like the way we use cash today. The only difference is that it relies on a complex computer network that depends heavily on cryptography (the science of secret writing) to verify and secure transactions, and also control the creation of new units.

Cryptocurrencies are one of the newest types of financial instruments available to trade. They are similar to currencies, however they are often discussed as coins and have a variety of different coins. Some of the types of cryptocurrencies are Ethereum, Ripple, Bitcoin Lite, and Bitcoin.

Just like currencies, nearly every experienced trader will tell you that beginners should not start with cryptocurrencies. In fact, most would probably see a beginner start with currency over cryptocurrencies. There are a couple main reasons for this one, both of them dealing with how risky these types of financial instruments are.

First, cryptocurrencies are newer and this means that there isn't as much research completed on them. In fact, one of the main things that experienced traders who are including cryptocurrencies in their portfolio are working hard to make sure they note everything about their trades so they can help expand the research on this type of financial instrument.

Second, cryptocurrencies are known to have high risk. They tend to suffer more than any other instrument when it comes to negative press, governmental regulations, and are even more likely to be hacked. Because of this, many traders feel it is important that the people who take on cryptocurrencies are comfortable with high risk, won't allow their mental state to be affected by the risk, and can remain calm under stress so they can continue to think rationally when having to make a quick decision to trade.

Futures

Futures are a good way to start your trading career. This is one of the most popular financial instruments among day traders but are also great for beginners who are looking to become swing traders. When you think of a future, you can think of an agreement between two people. A future is basically a contract that states exactly when stock will be sold. Typically, the agreement states that the stock will only be sold at a specific price. For example, both parties could agree that if the stock reaches $5, then the stock is to be sold. However, the stock cannot be sold to the second party until the price of $5 is reached.

Many people feel that futures are a great way to learn about the stock market. It decreases risk because you are able to create a contract that states this stock will be sold at a certain price. Of course, before you decide to agree to the contract, you will do all the research you need to do and make sure, to the best of your abilities, that you will end up with capital gain instead of a loss with the price you choose. Many beginners who state that they used futures within their first couple of months as a trader say they were able to get some more hands-on experience and learn about the stock market as they took part in futures. On top of that, they were able to gain pretty good profits.

Options

In the basic sense, options are similar to futures in there is a contract between two parties that states when the stock can be sold. However, instead of just focusing on the price, the agreement also focuses on a specific date. Furthermore, in order for the stock to become an option, there are four requirements that are needed.

1. The owner of the stock needs to agree upon the price. This process is known as the strike price.

2. You need to know the stock that the option is being applied to, such as IBM or MasterCard.

3. When it comes to options, buying is referred to as call and selling is referred to as put.

4. You also need to have a date of expiration for the option.

Like with any other type of financial instrument, there are positives and negatives associated with options. It is important to remember that all trades carry some sort of risk, no matter how well you try to manage the risk. This means that you can exhaust yourself making sure you have used every risk management technique that you can use and still have an amount of risk involved. Therefore, it is best to understand that sometimes you will lose on a trade and other times you will profit.

Forex

In simple terms, the Forex Market is nothing but a financial market, where people can trade currencies. If you are wondering what a financial market is, here is an explanation. A financial market is a place where buyers and sellers meet to exchange assets. Common assets that are traded in a financial market include stocks, bonds, currencies, commodities, options, derivatives, you name it.

The underlying principle of making profit in this market is that, if the currency you acquired, in this case, the British Pound increases in value against that of the Dollar, you make money. On the downside, if the opposite happens, you lose money. It is just as simple as that. Majority of the activity that takes place in the Forex Market during the weekdays is simply this; buying one currency in exchange of another.

Bond

As a matter of fact, the bond market is considered to be bigger than the stock market. In any event, the bond market is simply a financial market where large corporations and even the government ask for loans from the public so that they can repay them later with interest. A good way to think about it is: when you show up to the bond market to invest your money, you are basically loaning out your money to a large corporation or even the government so that they can pay it on a future date at a defined interest rate. This is very much the same way the bank lends you a loan, only that in this case, you are the bank. It is for this reason that bond investments are considered fixed-income investments.

Commodities

Another financial market that offers you an opportunity for trading or speculating is the commodities market.

The commodities are basically a financial market where buyers and sellers trade commodities. Commodities dealt in this financial market include agricultural goods such as cocoa, soy beans, wheat, cotton, rice and sugar. You also have raw materials like gold, silver, oil, copper, aluminum, lumber and gas being traded in this market.

In reality, when you trade in this market, you will not be buying and selling physical versions of these commodities. You will only be buying virtual gold or silver. Much of the activity that takes place in this market is speculative in nature, in that people will only be trading prices but on paper, you will have bought these commodities.

The way you speculate in this market is simply the same way you would trade any other market that we have just discussed. You could look at the price of wheat today or do your research and determine that in the future, there would be a shortage and therefore a high demand for it. This would imply that the price would rise in the near future.

You would then step in and purchase wheat and anticipate its price to go up. If you were right about the direction of price movement, you would make money when you sell later.

Conversely, you would do the opposite and sell if your analysis and research indicated a down price movement.

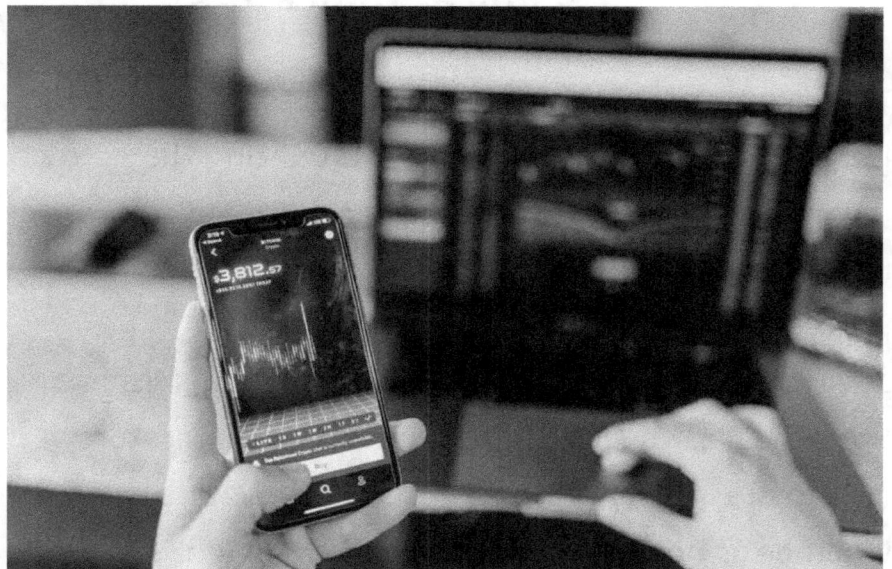

Chapter 5
Candlestick Chart Patterns and Technical Indicators

These patterns are really easy to detect when you're looking at candlestick charts while utilizing the correct technical indicator. Now, using technical indicators isn't always easy, but it's pretty much a 2-step process:

1. Apply Technical Indicators To The Price Of Your Stock- Here, you'll be applying technical indicators (which are simply math formulae) which will show you whether or not the stock is displaying buy or sell signals.

Technical indicators generally remove all subjectivity from analyzing a chart pattern. Technical indicators are one of two kinds- trending and non-trending.

- Trending technical indicators will show you the most significant changes in a given direction and mostly filter out the chart noise (irrelevant changes which don't contribute to the overall trend.) Now, this can easily happen over a few days, and the indicators will help measure the trends as well as signal when the trend is about to reverse, which will let you sell out at an ample time.

- Non-trending technical indicators tend to work with the buyers and sellers of a security. It determines how much the strength of the other investors in the market are affecting the stock movement. These indicators will often use a standardized price history by establishing the lowest and highest prices within a given time period. After that, they will be measuring the securities position in reference to that range. These indicators will also tell you when a stock is being over or under bought. When a stock is overbought that means it's overdue for a reversal in the trend, as the stock has risen too high. Oversold means the same thing but implies the stock will rise.

While you'll find that many swing traders are looking for the one system of indicators that will always give them the correct result that just doesn't exist. Unfortunately, every indicator can be wrong, swing trading isn't just a concrete science that will always give you profits. If it was everyone would do it, and more importantly, we'd use computer programs for it.

This is why fundamental analysis is so important, it helps you figure out when the technical indicators you're observing are actually correct, rather than simply leaving it to guesswork. You'll find that many swing traders will neglect fundamental analysis even though it is what can help you really get ahead of the market.

2. Compare the Stock to the Rest of the Overall Market- This step, also known as relative strength analysis involves the comparison of the performance of a stock to its market or industry. By looking at the disparity between these two, you'll be able to tell whether or not the stock you've chosen is performing good or bad.

Divergences are extremely good signals because they show you how well the stock of your choice is performing regardless of the way the industry, in particular, is performing.

The Wider View-Fundamental Analysis

If fundamental analysis sounds like a 9-headed hydra to you, and you aren't feeling very much like Heracles, don't be afraid. We'll be using the KISS approach to fundamental analysis in this book. Which is to say we'll "Keep It Simple Stupid."

Now, I'm not going to try to set you up for your MBA in economics. What I'm trying to do here is present you the actually important bits. That is to say that we'll be looking at the most important, key parts of a firm's fundamentals. Only those that affect stock prices are really important to us. After all, we're traders, not economists.

Fundamental analysis is about constantly asking questions. You'll be asking questions like how fast is this company growing, what is its position in relation to the competition, what about the returns?

Through repeatedly answering these questions over and over again, you'll begin to have an idea of what the company's shares should be trading at. Often, you'll find that they aren't trading at that point, which is where you make your entry.

You're not going to find the intrinsic value of a stock that institutions like Wall Street are trying to calculate (the intrinsic value is the true value of the company, rather than simply being the value that the market arrives at.) On the other hand, you don't need the intrinsic value. You're not trying to find the value of the shares down to a singular cent. On the other hand, if you determine their value is between $30 and $50 but they're trading at $20 then you don't need much more to invest.

Getting To Grips With Why It Works

There's much less debate on whether or not fundamental analysis works compared to technical analysis working. After all, the whole field of investing is rooted in it. The more a company earns the more people are willing to pay to have a share of it. Let's say you rent out an apartment for $500 a month, regardless of how much you think the true value of a $500 a month apartment is, it'll be half of the value of a $1000 apartment.

Naturally, fundamental analysis is a bit more complex than this in practice. You'll be looking at quarterly earnings rather than $500 or $1000 a month. The point, however, is that fundamental analysis tries to get the value of a company from its projected future earning potential.

Arbitrageurs are a vital component of why fundamental analysis works. They are generally looking for riskless profits for themselves. For example, if a share is, say $20 a pop, and the firm is valued at $1 billion, then if the firm has $2 billion on their bank, with no debt then an Arbitrageur will pop in and buy a ton of those shares.

The Arbitrageurs taking advantage of such miss-pricings is what helps the market stay afloat. The Arbitrageur might even buy the company for $1 billion and pay for it using the money that the company had on its pricing books.

The bottom line is- fundamental analysis works because entities such as investors, firms or governments pursue riskless profits endlessly.

How to Start Trading

In this chapter, I'll guide you through selecting a quality broker for yourself and opening a trading account. In addition to that, we'll be looking at service providers, starting a trading journal, as well as how to maintain a good mentality to succeed as one.

Brokers

Much like every other kind of trader, swing traders rely on brokers. On the other hand, a swing trader needs to use a different kind of broker from the rest of them. This will depend on a variety of factors we'll be going through in this chapter.

Those factors will be broken down step by step in this chapter, in addition to a variety of details needed to open a brokerage account. After you're done with that, all you need to do is grab a few services to conduct analysis for you.

While some services are useful for conducting market screening, others will chart stocks etc. It's important to decide how much you want to invest in your setup, and I'll recommend some quality services so you can make your pick based on your needs. In addition to this, we'll be making a trading journal, which is, as you'll soon find, one of the most useful tools for a trader out there.

Now, why is the firm that's executing all of your trades being called a broker? It doesn't precisely sound like the best of names and quite frankly sounds much shadier than it should. Brokers really aren't a complicated subject.

Even though their name sounds a bit intimidating, you need a broker in order to become a swing trader...or well, to be a trader in any capacity. On the other hand, due to the wonderful capitalistic market we have, not all brokers are the same. Some will give you highly customized advice while others specialize much more in wealth-management. Some of the highest net-worth people out there participate in these trades. After all, these brokers are quite worth it. Naturally, some of these higher-quality brokers will charge massive fees, because, well, they can simply afford to do it? Generally, they'd tell you that the massive fees they offer are reflective of their advice.

You don't need this. Well, unless you're a billionaire, in which case I think you already know all you need about trading. The brokers that use swing traders use are much lower costed. They are so called no-frill brokers. The good thing about these brokers is that due to competition, even they are giving ATM card access, check-writing privileges etc.

Now, with all of those factors, how do you pick one? The most common factor I see aspiring traders looking at is commissions. After all, nobody wants a broker to take any sum of their profits. This is a mistake.

Now, now, before you rush me down and put me on a pike, I am not trying to say they don't matter. Naturally, fees do matter. Swing trading wasn't even possible in the olden days due to the massive commissions that were everywhere.

Today, it's different. Fees these days really aren't that much, you'll be paying something like a flat $5-12 per trade that you make, which can easily be less than 0.1% of your trading volume. The difference between $5 and $12 isn't large to you, however, it might mean that you get some extra perks you otherwise wouldn't. Now, some of the other factors are:

- Charting systems- If you rely a lot on technical analysis when you're making your trades then you'll be wanting a broker that's good at charting. The charting quality and ease of reading can make the difference between success and failure.
- Customer service- In my opinion, this is the single most important factor to look at when selecting a broker. Keep in mind these are people that will be handling massive amounts of your money. You don't want to put it in the hands of someone who you can't properly reach when you need them. Every trader will also sometimes run

into problems with their broker, and in those times, this really counts.
- Ease of Deposits and Withdrawals- How easy it is to get money from your broker is only important when you're trading for a living. If it's hard, you won't have an easy time getting that monthly paycheck. On the other hand deposits are very important when making time-sensitive trades.

Which brokers you're going to choose also depends on how much you're planning to spend, fundamentally, there are two kinds of brokers:

1. Discount Brokers: These brokers are those that instead of offering quality and high-tier services, simply focus on executing trades. You tell them what you want bought and sold, they do that. Naturally, most of these trades will be made through the PC, unless you pay extra for phone support. These brokers are generally cheaper, and offer fewer services.

2. Direct access firms- Direct access firms are those companies that let you go past a broker and trade with an exchange or market without a middleman. The advantage of doing this is that you'll have way more control due to being able to see who's offering what and for how much.

Usually, these brokers will require you to get some software that will give you very high-speed data, usually superior to streaming sites. While some discount brokers are offering direct access trading, these are generally worse at it than dedicated companies.

2.5 Full Service Brokers- This isn't really on the list because it's not for you. These are brokers like Merrill Lynch, they will offer you a bazillion different services, and charge you just about as much. A swing trader shouldn't need anyone whispering down their ear about what trades to make. Swing trading is a road of independence, you don't need someone else telling you what trades to take and what trades you shouldn't take.

 I'm not going to recommend a single broker to you in this book, after all, the quality of brokers easily changes over time. Because of that, I can't really tell you which brokers are good or bad. On the other hand, I also can't know which country you're in, and while most of this book is US-driven, the fundamentals I want to apply everywhere. Just keep in mind to select quality brokers that offer everything you need!

You Need Some Standards Girl

Now, much like a girl that's just entered college, and is faced with the abundance of guys hitting on her, you'll need some standards to pick up the diamonds from the rough.

So, let me give you some baseline things to look for in a broker, like an older girl in a sorority.

Commissions: Never overpay, anything above $10 flat is a bit of a rip-off - that also shouldn't be more than 1-2c off of every share you're buying. Anything higher than this is pretty much just the broker preying on new people like you. It's also important to note that the higher your fees are, the more money you need to earn before you break even. While I've recommended some specific rates just now, too many people look only at rates and nothing else. That is the biggest noob trap in the whole world of trading, and there are a lot of noob traps. Commission rates are important but not as important as some other things.

Versatility: In this day and age, it's very important for your broker to offer to trade more securities than just stocks. Naturally, while most of us start off at stocks, trading other markets is also very popular. If your broker can figure out how to get you trading international securities, currencies etc. then that's a big plus. Naturally, you should be expecting to pay a small premium on top of the standard fee for services like this.

Various Banking Services: You'll find that some brokers are willing to give you services like check-writing or ATM transactions. These are generally just hassle-free measures to get your money. If you aren't trading seriously I'd recommend fetching one of these. With that being said, pretty much every broker will let you get your stuff to your PayPal card, so it shouldn't be all that hard getting your money.

Usability: This refers to your broker's UI and is possibly one of the most important thing about a broker. Think about it like looks in a guy, while they may not be the most important thing, everyone has a baseline of what they'll accept, and if he's pretty enough, most other things won't matter. Well, similarly to that, don't forget to check under the hood of the pretty ones, as they often don't contain everything else you need. On the other hand, a user-friendly and usable UI can make trading much easier, or even increase your profits. If it's quick and easy to place orders you're much less likely to get stressed out and make a bad trade or several. Also note that some brokers will let you test out a demo version of their platform before signing up.

Varied Amenities: Amenities are things that include services conductive to research and charting services. Let's give you an example, a discount broker may be willing to give you level 2 quotes- these will give you the access to order books for Nasdaq stocks. You will also get stock reports from Wall Street, as well as other research reports. On the other hand, these aren't really useful when swing trading due to the short-term nature of it.

Customer Service: This is the one thing I can't stress enough. It's the equivalent of a guy's core values. Sure, you can make do without them for a time, but after some time, you'll find that you're simply incompatible and nothing else can make up for them. It's very hard to determine how responsive a broker will be unless you rely on the internet, so check reviews and do a detailed analysis of every one of them when it comes to customer service. You want to be able to get your broker on the phone whenever you need them, rather than waiting for when it may be too late.

Reports and Analysis: This is the part of a broker that determines how well they can present you your data. Do they provide you year-to-date portfolio index returns? While sure, you could calculate this all yourself, having a broker do it is much easier. It's also great to have tax services in countries that have manual tax reports like the US.

The First Step-Opening An Account

After you've made your pick as to which broker you want to do business with, you'll need to decide on the kind of account you want to open with them.

Here you've got a variety of options, based on whether borrowing money to trade from your broker sounds appealing, as well as your position on trading futures or placing the account on your name or your spouse. You can even make the account a retirement account, or a traditional investing account. The next two questions will answer this, well except the spouse one, that one's to be had between the two of you...I'm not good at relationship counseling.

Cash Or Margin Account

Whether you want to get a cash or margin account will depend on you after selecting, which broker you, want to do business with. When you get this choice, keep in mind that cash restricts you to trading with funds you have available, while margin accounts allow you to borrow from your broker to trade. Picking an account is also necessary if you want trading options.

A swing trader with say, $30 000 can borrow up to $30 000 usually, now, this is a double edged sword. Let's say you invest all of it...and you lose 10%, instead of losing 3000 you'll be losing 6000 due to the money you borrowed. Margin accounts tend to make traders much more reckless. By being allowed to trade with money that isn't really yours the dealership is trying to get you to pay a fee on the money you borrowed. These can easily lead to you getting in way over your head.

If you're a new trader (as you probably are) you should be sticking exclusively to cash accounts.

Traditional Vs Retirement Account

The second account division is traditional and retirement. The difference is really quite self-explanatory.

Now, the biggest difference here is well, taxes. Traditional accounts will let you take your money whenever you want, and however much of it you want to take out. On the other hand, they also mean that you have to report this as taxable income. In the US at least, if you get classified as a full time trader you can make less taxes by turning these gains from capital to ordinary. This is important because if you aren't classified as a full time trader then you're going to have to pay the full capital tax.

A retirement account stops these problems, however, the government doesn't like this idea, and hence stops you from putting as much money as you'd like into it. Your IRA caps out at $5000 a year if you're under 49. The government also limits you when it comes to taking that money out, in most countries you can only do it after turning 59.

These kinds of inconveniences tend to be why people elect to not open a retirement account. If you just want to max out your retirement, then opening a retirement account is definitely the best idea.

Picking A Service Provider

Unfortunately, trading without a service provider is pretty much impossible. On the other hand, these are all different from each other, so a newbie might get overwhelmed by choice when selecting them.

These differ in a few ways but mainly its timelines, quality, and breadth of data that makes the final decision. What you want in one of these is all the services that you need. Primarily, you'll want charting and access to a database. You'll need those to conduct both technical and fundamental analysis. Now we're going to go over the main things you'll want to look for in a service provider.

Now, let's sit down and take a short lesson on the service provider business model first. They make money by making a deal with a data provider, and then providing you with the data that is relevant for you.

Service providers will be giving you the tools to find and chart the stocks that you want, which will increase the amount of info you have on the market. Using tools such as these is flexible enough to let you change all of your inputs. Ranging from what indicators to use to which criteria to pay attention to.

Providers are classified into two main categories. You've probably guessed it, it's those that provide technical data, and those that provide fundamental data. Those that provide both are therefore classed as unicorns.

A strong charting system is, well, pretty much necessary if you want to be a successful swing trader. They simply do way too much for you to be successful without them. That isn't to say it's straight-up impossible, but it will be far more difficult compared to just taking a provider and going with it.

You will absolutely require real time charts and quotes. Real time here means that they are of live market data, and are not being delayed by an external cause. If your plans are to trade interday, then when you enter your orders, you don't really need real time charting. After all, you'll be entering orders after-market hours. The market has a ludicrous amount of charting providers, and most of these cater to the active traders that are in their system. This is to say that most discount brokers will have connections with some charting systems. In fact, order entry is often integrated with charting, allowing you to make automatic buys and sells, which is a great feature.

While there are a lot of excellent charting services online, I can't really recommend any off the tip of the hat, because I don't know what country you're in and what the rules there might be. With that being said, I would check it out online and then determine if you need additional charting.

Now, charting systems themselves can be difficult to select from. After all, every provider will try to make themselves look different. Spoiler alert: Most of them aren't all that different. All you need to do is pay attention to what you need, the primary concern will be ease of use. After all, you won't have all day to fish out charts, you need them to be available pretty much at the snap of your fingers. Consider their visual appeal and clarity as well, you don't want to spend hours on just reading a chart.

Features such as being able to input your own indicators are excellent for advanced traders. If your plan is to stick with a single one for all of your career, then try to look for one that lets you insert custom indicators. You'll be thanking me later.

When it comes to selecting these programs I recommend checking the rankings made by Technical Analysis of Stocks & Commodities in its yearly Reader's Choice Awards. I use two charting systems: one, which is specially provided by my broker and another one in which I make the bulk of my personal research.

Fundamental analysis software lets traders who decide upon using fundamental analysis in investing as a process need to get a subscription to data providers that can assist them in their research.

It's lucky that most of a company's fundamental data, ranging from historical earnings to expected growth, is available... for free... online, God bless the internet. Honestly, it's amazing how far trading has come, and how easy it is to come across this stuff online these days.

Like seriously, just open Google Finance and look at all it gives you. Ten years ago, my broker couldn't have given me that much information. And this is all FREE, in this age of digitalization, it's important to remember that most of the things you need are available online, if you know how to look for it.

- The balance sheet of the company you're looking at

This and many other things are all available for free. Beware, though, that it does have a message board. Run away from those, for reasons we'll discuss soon, you don't want to be getting into any message boards just yet (or, well, ever really.)

Reuters is another site you can use. While sites like Yahoo! and Google will give you aggregate data, Reuters makes its own data. The main categories available on the website are Stock Overview, Financial Highlights, Estimates, Officers and Directors, Financial Statements, Recommendations, and Analyst Research. All of these have some of their uses, though as a swing trader you'll be primarily looking at Ratios.

The excellent thing about this site is the variety of data it provides. It will give you data on a company vs its peers as well as other things. Such as whether the company is going through good or bad times, as well as free research services. On the other hand, the paid subs are also quite great.

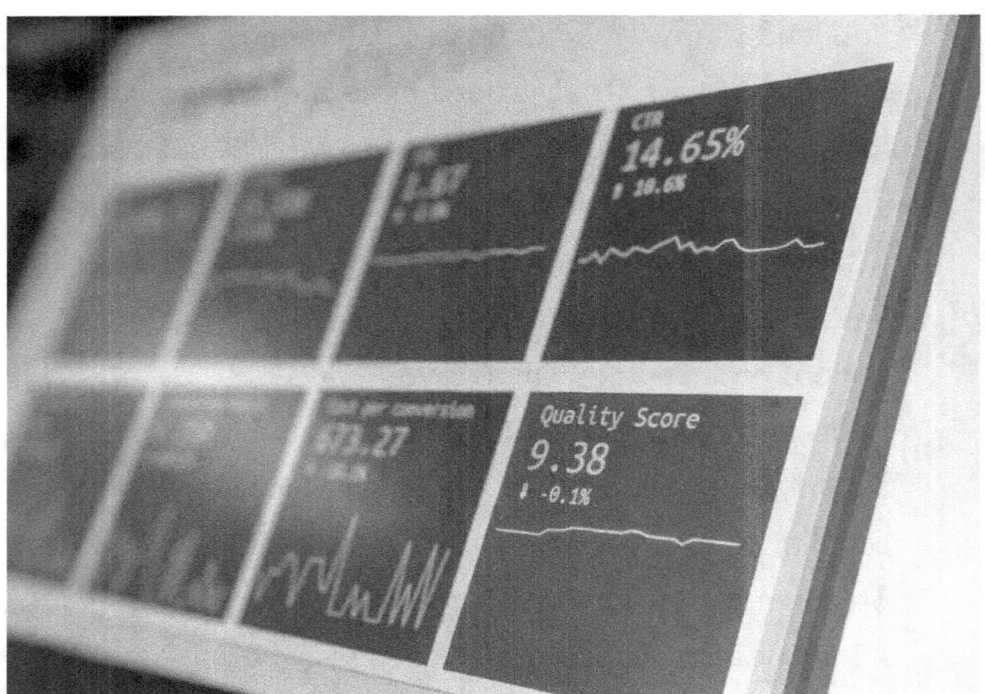

Chapter 6   Swing Trading Rules

Swing trading can take some time to master. It is easier to work with compared to working with day trading, but it is much harder and requires a lot of patience and time commitment compared to working with some of the longer-term investments that you can choose. Despite this extra work, there is the potential for you to make a big profit with limited risk if you follow the right rules. This chapter will take some time to look at some of the rules that you need to see success when it comes to swing trading.

Align the trade with the market

When you are trying to figure out what trades to do, you always need to take a look at what the market is doing. The market is not going to behave in the manner that you would like, so you need to learn how the market is about to behave and then pick your trades to go with that.

The overall direction the market will take will be measured through the S&P 500. These trends will provide you with some context for making your short-term trades. Remember that short-term trades will be a bit different than you will find with long-term trends and look at how the market will behave in the next few weeks is more important than worrying about how the market will do over the next few years.

However, you also do need to pay some attention to the trends that happen over the long-term with swing trading. These trends will often show up again and again for a particular stock and take a look at them can help to increase your profit potential. Yes, it is important to take a look at the short-term and see what is going on with the market to see if anything is about to change and then trade along with that trend. The more you can look at the charts, both long-term and short-term the more you will be able to make good decisions on your trades.

Go short weakness and long strength

You should not avoid or fight off the tape once you figure out what the overall trend is. You need to look at the charts to find long trades that will work during periods of bullishness. And then when you are dealing with periods of bearishness, you need to find the right short trades. These trends will help you to get the results that you would like when it comes to successful swing trading.

Enter at the beginning rather than the end

One mistake that some beginners will make is that they will try and enter the trend near the end of it, rather than catching the trend at the beginning. This will limit some of the money that you can make if you wait too long to enter into a trend. Of course, it is much better to get into the market at some time for the trend, before it goes down because you will be able to make some money, but the earlier you can get into the trend, the more money you can make.

When looking at the charts, it is important to look for early signs of the change. The earlier you can see these new trends, the less risk you will take with swing trading and the bigger the profits you will make. This means that you have to be active. Trends can go quickly and if you are not careful about what is going on in the market, and you are not looking at the market averages, you will end up missing out on some trends and will miss out on some money, or even lose money.

Looking at the overall market averages on your charts will help out with this. When you look at the market averages, you will sometimes see that the stocks have been oversold or overbought. When this has happened, it means that it is likely they will turn around again soon. If the trend looks like it is about to reverse, you can jump in, get the stock for a good price, and sell it over the next few weeks when things start to go back up.

You need to get some of your own indicators in place to figure out when these trends are about to happen. The Volatility Index, the Put/Call Ratio, and the Arms Index are good tools. You will be able to see, through these methods, when the market is testing a major zone of resistance and support, and it can help you to predict what will happen in the future.

On the other hand, looking at moving average crossovers and trendlines will make you fall behind. These are just going to confirm that a trend is happening and by the time you see them and join in on a trade, it may be too late to make any money. These tools can help you determine if you have made a good decision along the way, but if you are relying solely on them, you will miss out.

Never trade on one technical concept

With swing trading, things will change on a frequent basis. You need to work with trading quickly, picking up one trade and then selling it within a few weeks. You do not get the benefit of staying with the market for a very long time, or you are missing out on the profits you can make. Relying on just one technical concept will lead you to a lot of trouble along the way.

In most cases, the highly profitable trades will occur when you can find at least two (but more is much better) technical tools send you the same message. There are times when several of your tools will show the same indicators, and this means that the stock will rise or fall sharply in the near future. This is great news for you. The more indicators that show the same information, the more likely that the trend is about to occur and that you will make a large profit in the process.

However, there are times when one indicator will show that a trend is about to occur. If you only look at that one indicator, you may find out after entering the trade that it is wrong. You want to have at least a few indicators in place to help you make your decisions. The best opportunities for swing trading will show up in at least a few indicators, and when you can get three or more of these to show up with the same message over a two or three day period, this will increase your profitability.

Enter the trade with a good plan

There are a lot of different strategies and plans that you can go with. Many of them can be successful when it comes to swing trading, but you do need to pick out a good one and stick with it. One of the worst things that a beginner can do is get started with a strategy, see that it is maybe not doing as well as they had hoped, and then skipping over to a new strategy right in the middle of their trade. This is setting yourself up for failure, and you are more likely to lose money with this method than any other.

It is fine to switch out the types of strategies that you want to use if you find one is not the best for you. But you must make sure that you pick out a strategy and use it for the whole time of your trade. Even if the trade is not going the way that you would like, stick with the strategy. This will limit your risks, and you will learn more from the experience in the long run. If a strategy is not the right one for you, simply switch to a different one the next time.

Try to work the odds

You are not able to make the market work the way that you would like. The market will behave however it would like. There are a lot of different people who are in the market, and the swing trading will only take place over a few days. You need to learn how to work with the market, rather than trying to influence it.

It is never a good idea to risk a dollar just so you can make a dime. You have to pick out smart trades, trades that will lower your risk as much as possible while making your high profits. There will be some trades that may promise a lot of money if you try them, but the risk is so high that you are likely to lose all of your investment plus more without making anything.

The best trades that you can do are ones that will provide you with a strong profit if you make the right types of decisions, but where you can limit your losses as much as possible if you are wrong. The profits may not be as big as some of the trades that you can make, but it ensures that you will not lose out on all your investment either.

Learn to control the emotions a little bit

The most important thing that you can do when you get into swing trading is learning how to keep your emotions out of the game. This is important no matter which investment you choose, but it is especially important when you are working with some of these short-term investments. Once your emotions get into the mix, it is a lot harder to make smart decisions and smart trades that will lead to profits.

If you let your emotions get into the mix, you are likely to make poor trading decisions. You will make decisions that will lead you to lose money. You will stay in the market too long, hoping to earn more money, or hoping that you can recover some of your losses. Basically, when you start letting the emotions get into the mix, you are risking your money, and you will end up losing out on all your hard work.

For those who are not able to think through their decisions critically, who are not able to keep their emotions out of the trades that they will do, it is much better to just stay out of the market completely. Swing trading needs some fast decision making and the help of a lot of research. If you are not able to do this without all the emotions, you will fail in the long run.

Do your trading with a consistent group of stocks

When you first get started with day trading, it is pretty easy to jump around between stocks. You may find on that looks good and then want to jump to another once the trade is all done. There is nothing wrong with following the action, but it is always best to have your core stocks that you track on a regular basis and learn how they work.

Having a few regular stocks is a great way to see regular success with swing trading. These regular stocks will allow you to learn about the market better and can save a lot of time researching. You will have time to learn how the stocks work and understand how they have performed in the past and are likely to perform in the future. It takes some of the work out of it all when you can stick with a few core stocks over the long term.

Of course, there is nothing wrong going with a new stock on occasion if you see some big trends that are coming up. This can be a great way to increase your profit, especially if you have been in the market for some time. But chasing after those new stocks can take up a lot of work. Learn as much about your core stocks as possible, and you will save a lot of work, reduce your risk, and increase your profits.

Everyone will spend time working with different methods and strategies when it comes to swing trading. And even with different methods, it is possible to see many people make a profit. If you follow some of these rules and learn how to pick the right strategy, you will see some great results when it comes to swing trading.

Swing trading is an extraordinary way to make cash for the initiators. It is straightforward and learns. You need to learn it by following four basic rules with the end goal to get well on the way to get the best stocks for swing trading with success. Swing trading is a procedure of trading that trusts on the getting responses among the significant trends which will be either upside trend or drawback trend. This trading, as a rule, goes on for around 2-5 days in a stream. Numerous Forex traders swing trade on the daily edges. It is unsafe so don't think to attempt it.

You need to pursue four rules with the end goal to taste success:

Rule 1: Use Support and Resistance

At whatever point you are trading you should discover the territories of help and resistance on the daily Forex graph. The ones which are high on the unpredictability are great that is because they slant not to keep going longer. For this, you should use the Bollinger band and also the trend lines.

When you are trading in Forex, never make this regular blame:

A few traders sit tight at the time when the cost will reach close to the point they are expecting and believe that by then of time they will enter the trade and seek after better levels of hold. Never foresee anything or figure anything because it will prompt a snappy wipeout and the market will remove your value and won't give you any prizes.

Rule 2: Watch Momentum

If you are en route to swing trade in Forex or any money related hardware, it underpins the trading sign. There is no additional space to grasp the individual pointers. That is the reason you should start with the stochastic and Relative Strength Index (RSI). Presently you are in the way of trading.

Rule 3: Set a Target

When you enter the trade, the benefits and misfortunes come at a quick pace. You can put the stop component which is anything but difficult to apply and is obligatory. It is at the posterior of the help and resistance that you are anticipating. If you are utilizing a stop close premise at that point put the objective just before when you figure the price will go as indicated by your desires. It is encouraged to go for a basic short swing trading framework whether you are a tenderfoot or an accomplished trader or speculator. This swing trading programming causes you to track your short swing trading stocks at a superior rate than you could do.

Rule 4: Shop Spreads

While you are engaged with swing trading stock, you will trade with unstable and fluid monetary forms. In the main segments, you should be skilled to get some stupefied spreads and that addition of a few pips as it were. Every one of the intermediaries is never comparative at whatever point it goes to the spreads. You should make astute choices because if the managing costs climb up, then you need to have the tightest spreads that are workable for you.

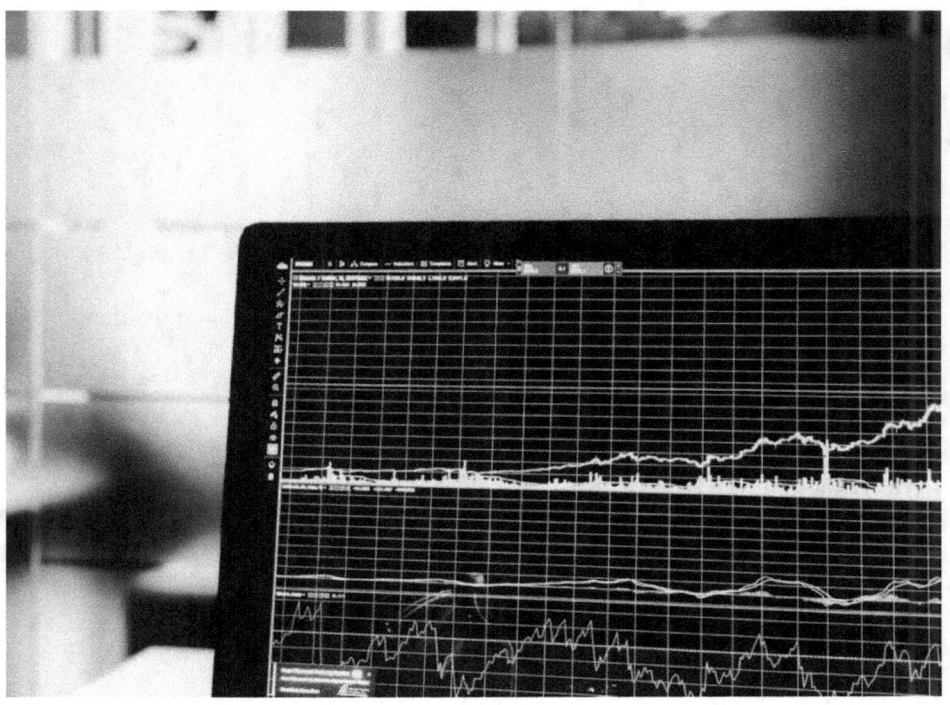

Chapter 7
Fundamental and Technical Analysis

Fundamental and technical analysis are both techniques used by investors and traders all around the world to make decisions on the stock market. In this chapter, we are carefully analyzing the two, their differences, similarities, and where they are best used.

Fundamental Analysis

Fundamental analysis is whereby the trader, stock analyst, or investor looks at the basic fundamental financial level of business when analyzing the trade. It analyzes the trades' profits, revenues, margins, earnings, losses, among others. This analysis determines the financial health of the trade by analyzing the trades' key rations. You can have an idea of stocks in a company through fundamental analysis. it accounts for several factors; these include asset management, revenue management, the interest rates as well as the production of the trade. The goal of fundamental analysis is to identify and determine the stocks' current worth and market value.

In fundamental analysis, you measure a stock or any type of security intrinsic value. This is done by studying all possible factors that influence the value of the stock, such as the financial management condition of the company and economic conditions. A particular value is then produced and compared against the current price to help the trader figure out if he or she will buy or sell any security. The stock is considered to be overpriced if the value is lower than the current price. While the stock is labeled undervalued if the value is more than what is the current price. Fundamental analysis involves going through both the tangible and intangible aspects of the trade. They are grouped into two aspects, the quantitative and qualitative fundamentals.

Quantitative fundamentals

The numeric characters that are measurable in a trade operation are known as quantitative fundamentals. They are obtained from the trade's financial statements, the profits, losses, revenues, and other assets. The cash flow statement, the balance sheet, and income statements. From these statements, you are able to analyze the financial status of the trade, where you are losing or gaining money.

Qualitative fundamentals

These are the intangible aspects of the trade. These are a competitive advantage, the competitive edge, the trades approach, the management quality, and the overall growth of the trade.

Limitations On Fundamental Analysis

If the management has wrongly recorded the financial details or they are was a misinterpretation, there is a great percentage that the decision you will make will be wrong as it will be based on false information, irrelevant, and data that is not accurate.

There is blind and total reliance on historical financial data to predict the future. This overreliance can prove to be fatal for the trade. Analysis should be done on recent changes in the trade and according to well predicted financial data.

Has over-ambitious, achievable assumptions that may lack the credibility of management and the industry growth areas. Assumptions may be based on future interest rates, growth rates, and other different factors. When these expectations and estimations are not archived, your whole investment can collapse.

Their prizes set on stocks might be influenced by overenthusiasm and can be set to a level that is not justified fundamentally. This can be dangerous for the trade. The fundamental analyst does analyze the business but not the stock market. There is no connection between the trades stock behavior and the progress of a stock.

Technical Analysis

The technical analysis evaluates investments and identifies opportunities by statistical analysis of tends from trading activities. These traded include volume and price movements. technical analysis majorly focuses on the trading signals, price movements, and other analytical charting tools. They are used to evaluate the securities weakness of strengths.
It uses trading data that is from past trades and price changes of security. These include futures, commodities, stocks, fixed income currencies. These are used as indicators of price movements of future securities.

Assumption Of Technical Analysis

There are two basic assumptions forming the framework for technical analysis.

The first assumption is that the market makes a discount on almost all things. There is criticism that technical analysist ignores the fundamental factors and only consider price movements. Technical analysts believe that everything is already prized to the market, from the broad market, the market psychology, and the trades fundamentals. This cancels out consideration of other factors when making an investment decision and only leaves out an analysis of price movements.

Secondly, the technical analyst believes rather than the stock price moving erratically; it is most likely to continue with past trends. This is because of the move in the long term, medium-term, and short-term trends. Most technical analysis is based on this assumption.

The market psychology tends to attribute to the repetitive nature of the prize movements; the trends tend to be very predictable. the technical analyst uses historical charts pattern to analyze previous market movements to have a clear understanding of the trades. They have a belief that history does repeat itself and that the prize movements will too.

Most traders buy and see stocks on the same day; they need to make quick decisions on the sale and purchase price. Using fundamental analysis is not possible when making such short-term decisions hence technical analysis being more preferred. This is because it helps the trader with ideas and directions of the stock price.

It should be noted that technical analysis is built on several assumptions and ignores other major factors. It focuses on the prediction of the price movements, which may not always be accurate and on point.

Limitations On Technical Analysis

The efficient market hypothesis tends to disapprove of the legitimacy of the technical analysis. it states that there is a reflection of all current and past information on the market prices, so there is no way you can use the patterns to your advantage to earn extra profit. Fundamental analysts and economists do not believe that prizes repeat themselves; rather, they move in as random movement and information contained in volume data, and the historical market cannot impact the trade.

It has been stated that technical analysis works sometimes because it is a self-fulfilling prophecy. A technical analyst can manipulate their ways of making sure that the market favors them. For instance, if many technical traders place a stop-loss order below a certain range and a larger number of traders do so with a similar range, the stocks will reach this price, increasing the number of sales orders pushing the stock down, making confirmation of the anticipated movement of the traders. Other traders will see the decrease in prize and sell their positions, making the trend stronger.

Difference Between Fundamental And Technical Analysis

The purpose of technical analysis is to focus on the internal market statics, the historical price movements, and patterned charts on such data, while the fundamental analysis focuses on the variable when making decisions on the trade. It shares prices based on financial statements, company statics, and facts. Each system of analysis has a preferred term. For short term investment decisions, you can use technical analysis due to the short-term trends and prize changes. such investors are more interested in short term profits as they buy and keep stocks for a short period of time, a couple of years probably. While fundamental analysis is mainly used by an investor who wants to make investment decisions that are long term. This is used for a project that will last for a longer time. They purchase stocks with largely laid out dividends payouts and hold the stocks for several years before selling them.

The fundamental analysis makes intrinsic value estimates for the purchase and shares; then, sales are made when the market surpasses these values. On the other hand, the technical analyst does not make value on a stock as they believe that it is all dependent on the demand and supply from the market. The market is lead through rational and irrational factors.

The past trends or prize fluctuations do not concern the fundamentalist, technicians rare; however, affected by these trends and price fluctuations, they do believe that they reoccur. they use charts to follow to prize movements and draw conclusions from them. There are no assumptions of similar prize trends in a fundamental analysis like in technical techniques.

In fundamental analysis, decision making is through analysis of financial statements, quality management, and growth trends. They are used to make judgments based on their statistical information. Technical analysts pay more attention to pattern charts indicating prize movements and the market trends.

To properly identify the overvalued and undervalued prizes of the stocks, you use the fundamental method of analysis as it compares the intrinsic value of the stocks and the market value while the technical method of analysis is more useful in checking and calculating which is the best time to bus of sell orders. There is a lot of investment in technical analysis. Millions are used to purchase and maintain technical analysis tools and trading software. This can be a bit difficult for the average individual trader. It is much cheaper to invest in fundamental analysis strategies.

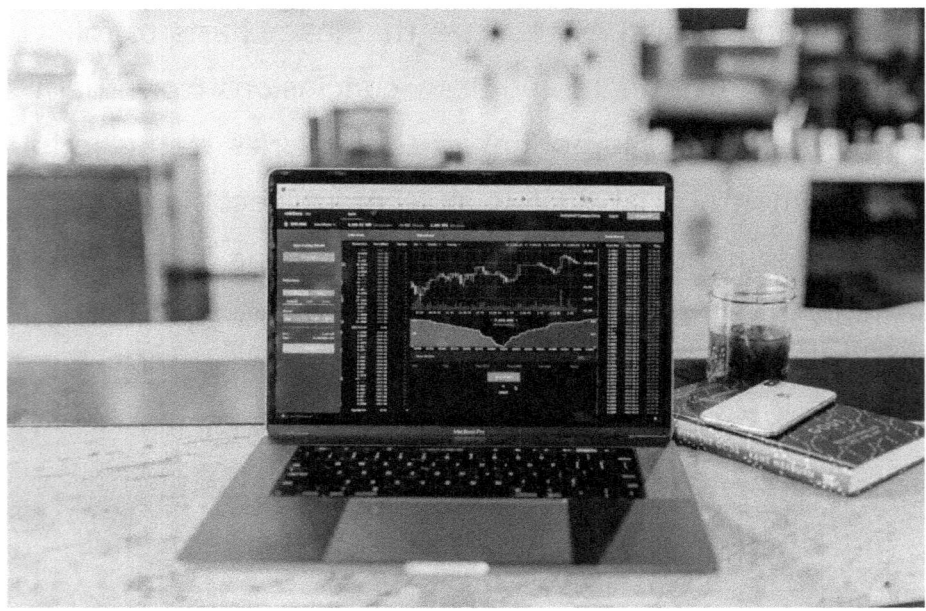

Chapter 8   Money Management

This term is used to refer to the process of investing, spending, saving, and budgeting; it is also used to refer to the way capital is used for personal or group usage. The other words used for money management includes portfolio and investment management. When you are good with money, it involves a lot apart from just meeting your needs. When it comes to money management, having math skills is not mandatory, there are different skills needed that will be discussed later.

Money management is simply how you handle all the finances and how you handle all your long-term goals. It also involves how an individual manages their investment in order to make great profits. Most people think that great money management skills are all about saying no when you are tempted to make a purchase. What it really implies is when you are able to say yes to what is important to purchase. When you do not practice good money management skills, whatever money you have might look little for your lifestyle.

To have a good start when it comes to money management, you need to know where you are. This is in terms of your financial capability and power; like assets and liabilities. Assets include your investment and bank accounts, any properties and retirement accounts. Liabilities are the things that you need to pay like credit card balances, any loans like student loans and car loans and any mortgages and outstanding debts. Your net worth is when the value of your assets is more than your liabilities. And when your liabilities are more than your asset that is considered a net loss or negative net worth. When you have great money management skills and approaches, getting a net worth will be easy.

Ensure that you set your goals in order to achieve great money management. Your goals will create a plan on how you will manage your money. When you have your goals set, it will give clarity on which are priority expenses and which you can let go. You will need discipline and effort in order to achieve all your efforts. For instance, when you plan to buy a car worth $20k, you will need to work harder and smarter and reduce your expenses. You will need to do all that as compared to someone whose budget car is $10k.

When you have your budget drafted and set, remember to have adjustments. When you prepare a budget, you have the chance to know all the expenses that you have. For instance, you can set aside $150 that can be for entertainment and any miscellaneous expenses after payment of all expenses and managing your debts. Good advice is when you get a pay increment, do not use the additional income for your entertainment but add it into your savings.

When you have a target to meet different goals, you are likely to have the money in different multiple accounts. A good example will be to ensure that you have a separate emergency fund so as not to get tempted for any impulse buying in the future. You will also have different strategies and that will be for different goals. You will be aggressive when you start investing in different stocks that you will not need to invest money in like 20 years. You need to also have an account that has no risks like a savings account that that can be used as emergency funds when the need arises. When you have such multiple accounts, you can use a software program to help in tracking the several accounts. A good one can be Quicken; it will track all your expenses and the savings goals.

The Basics of Money Management

Money management is a term that deals with solutions and services that are in the investment field. The good thing is, in the financial market there are different resources available that can help in personal financial management. For any investor, their intention is to have a good net worth, so it will come a time when they will need the services of professionals like financial advisors. The advisors are known to offer brokerage services, money management plans, and private banking. The advice is best for retirement, estate planning and other benefits.

When you are in business, it seems complicated when there is a need to manage cash flow and different accounts. When you are able to strike a balance, you are guaranteed to be successful. If you are not able to manage all that, you will need to get the services of an accountant or bookkeeper to do all that for you. Even if you will outsource, you need to know the basics of money management and bookkeeping. You will need to know simple tasks like interpreting bank statements, understanding accounts payable and receivable, credit, and tax forms.

Money management will also involve knowing more about debit cards, checks, online payments, cash, and credit cards when it comes to payment options in your business. You will also need to have a planned and established payment plan and a debt collection system just in case of non-payment.

Opening a bank account is another way to help in money management, you need to choose a name and have an operating and registered business. Make sure you get more information on credit card facilities, a debit account, and any other additional services.

Another important concept is to ensure that you have extended credit facilities in case of late payments. This can be planned for 30-6-90-120 days after a product is delivered or a service is rendered. You can motivate your customers to pay on time by extending discounts. Before the credit extension, ensure that you have done proper background check especially with large amounts. Even when there is credit extension, there are times where you will end up not being paid or not aid in time. To be able to recover your money, you need to ensure there is open and clear communication.

What Are Money Management Skills?

Before you can know of the best skills for money management, you will need to ask yourself some questions. What is your weekly or monthly income? Do you have a list of expenses that you need to pay? What you need to know is that money management is a skill used in life and cannot be taught in school. These skills cannot be learned in school but mostly from life experience.

- ✔ Have the ability to set a budget. This will help in tracking your expenses and the way you spend money. What do you spend a lot on, is it entertainment, clothes, or food? What is the tendency of overdrawing money from your bank account? If all that is yes, then you will need to set a budget. Look at your monthly statement and write down all the expenses in categories. You will be surprised by how much you are wasting.

✔ Spend what you have wisely. Always have a shopping list when you go shopping. Do you have a habit of looking at the product prices before putting it in the shopping basket? If you have coupons, ensure you use them. There are mobile apps and online resources that can help in focusing on your expenses. Do you know how to monitor your expenses? When you are not attentive to this advice, you will end up losing your hard-earned money.

✔ Always balance your books, do not always have a tendency of getting your bank balance online. When you depend on online information, there will be an issue when you want to know the balance on what you are spending at that particular moment. Be accountable and ensure you record all your expenses and this will help in avoiding any over-spending.

✔ Set a plan that will help in accomplishing anything that you put your mind. When you have a financial plan, you will be able to track how you are spending your money.

✔ Always think like an investor. When in school, you will not be taught how to handle money but largely on how to invest your money and have wealth growth. Learn to grow your savings and to invest at an early age. Turn that $100 to $200, $400, $800, and more. Having a stable financial future means that you have invested and grown in your money. When you start thinking like an investor, your money will grow. If you have a spouse or partner ensure that, they also know about your financial goals. If you possess a joint account with your partner or spouse, always work together and agree on the financial goals. When you are stuck or in doubt, consult a financial adviser and learn a lot of how to invest.

✔ Save your money, always be focused, and committed when it comes to saving money and this will guarantee a better future. This will help in improving your financial positi0n and even make it better. The first step is to have the decision to do that and this will help improve your management skills.

Importance of Money Management

Money management will help any individual in living on a budget and within their means. You will be able to look for great bargains and avoid any deals you believe that is not good when making a purchase. When you start getting a stable income, you will need to know how to invest because that will help in attaining your goals. And when you practice proper money management, you will meet all your goals and plans. There is the importance of money management:

✔ You will have better financial security: When you are careful with your expenses and savings, you will end up having enough for your future. Your savings will help in giving the proper financial security and you will be able to take care of yourself in case of emergencies. With your savings, you will not need to use your credit card in case of any issues.

✔ When you have proper money management and manage to save, you will be able to get opportunities and invest in the business. It will be frustrating to know of a great opportunity and not having enough funds to invest.

✔ Your credit scores will be determined by the way you manage your money. When you have high credit, score means you have managed to pay your bills on time and you have low-level debt. A high credit score means you will have more savings and you will be charged low interest when making purchases like cars or mortgages.

✔ Money management helps in reducing stress, this will happen when you start paying your bills on time. When you are late in paying your bills, you will encounter stress. Stress will bring about health problems like insomnia, migraines, and hypertension. You need to be aware of how you will handle money management, this will help in having extra cash and manage to save and manage a stress-free life.

✔ Money management helps in earning more money and when your income increases, you need to develop proper budgeting. And know of the right places to invest the extra money you have made. You need to know of additional venues to save money like in stocks and mutual funds; this will help in earning more money unlike money laying in your savings account. Ensure you learn about the investments, not all investments are profitable. The better thing about investments is that you can be on a monthly salary and still earning from your investment.

✔ When you adapt great money management skills, you will not waste money on unnecessary things. When you do not know how you are spending your income, it will be easy to be in debt. When you use your spare time effectively, it will help in managing your money. For instance, when you spend time with your friends and family members, ensure that you are aware of your budget.

✔ Peace of mind is guaranteed when you have better money management skills. When you a stable income and better savings, you will be able to handle any financial issues with confidence that all your needs can be handled perfectly.

World Top Money Managers

These managers are known to offer management and investment advice. They manage both active and passive funds.

✔ The Vanguard Group: It is a well-known management and investment firm, they have more than 20 million clients and in more than 100 countries. They started in Pennsylvania in the '70s and they have grown their assets to more than $5 trillion by close of 2018. They hold over 300 funds, move 150 in the US and more than 400 indexes to all of their market funds.

✔ Pacific Investment Management Company: This management firm has a worldwide presence and founded in California in the '70s. They have grown their asset base to more than $1 trillion by close of 2018. They have over 700 professional managing investments and with over 10 years as experts. They have over 100 funds and they lead in the fixed income sector.

- BlackRock, Inc: They started with their main company as BlackRock Group, by 1988 they started another division and labeled it BlackRock, Inc. They grew their assets to over $15 billion in 5 years and by the end of 2018, they grew to over $6 trillion and they have become the largest company in investment management in the world. They have over 100k in their workforce and over 50 offices in more than 30 countries. More than 20% of their assets are equivalent to $16 trillion.
- Fidelity Investments: This firm was founded in the '40s and by end of 2019 their customers have grown to over 20 million and more than $5 trillion in asset base. Their mutual fund is more than 300, this includes domestic and foreign equity, money market, fixed income, money markets and allocation of funds.

✔ Invesco Ltd: This firm has been in business since 1940 in offering investment advice. They announced in 2018, that they have made over $800 billion way above their products. They have over 100 EFTs that are made from their share capital. In 2017, they had a decline and it affected their stock price. They have managed to be among the best in the world despite all the challenges and setbacks. They have become among the top and best companies in the world, in terms of money, assets, and investment management.

The Approaches Used in Money Management

Great financial skills make money management easier, and how our money is spent largely affects your credit score and your debt cycle. There are tips that can help you if you are struggling with how to manage your money.

✔ Always have a Budget: Most people do not like to have a budget because they believe it is a boring and repetitive process. That involves listing all their expenses, summing up numbers, getting everything up, and running. When you have a budget, there is less room to be bad with money. You will get to know your income and expenses. The secret is focusing on the value that the budget will bring to your life instead of the budget creation process.

✔ After making the budget, the trick is to make sure that you use your budget. It will be a waste of time when you draft a budget and you do not stick to it. If it is a weekly or monthly budget, ensure that you refer to it often, and it will help when making your spending decisions. The budget should be made in a way that, at any given time you can easily track how much you have spent and know of any penning expenses.

✔ When drafting your budget, have a limit set for any unbudgeted expenses. In any budget, what is important to know is the funds left after paying all your expenses. When you have any budget and everything is settled, you can have the balance for your entertainment purposes. The amount set for fun should be a specific amount from your income. If you are planning to have a big purchase, refer to your budget first.

✔ Start by tracking your spending habits. When you have small purchases, they will end up piling and finally, you will notice that you have gone beyond your budget. When you track your spending plans. you will be able to know the places that you are failing and how you can rectify them. If you can, ensure that you save all your receipts and have a record of your spending in a journal. Have them in categories so that you can easily track them and know of the areas that are hard to stick on a budget.

✔ When your income is steady and qualifies you for a credit facility that does not mean that you should get that facility. You do not need to commit yourself to any monthly recurring bill. Most people think that the bank will not approve of the facility because they cannot afford it. What the bank knows is just your income exactly as you have reported. And if you have given a credit report, they will use what is offered on that report and they will not have any obligations not to give the credit facility. It is a personal decision to know if you qualify for the credit facility and if you have the capability to pay regarding your monthly income and other obligations.

✔ When making a purchase decision, ensure that you are paying the right and best prices. The best way to do this is by making a comparison and making sure that you are paying the lowest prices for the products and any services rendered. Look for discounts, cheaper alternatives, and coupons.

✔ In situations whereby you are planning to make a huge purchase, ensure that you save for that purchase. When you have the ability to delay gratification, will help in ensuring that you manage your money in a better way. It is advisable to out of large purchases, instead of sacrificing important things or tying a purchase to a credit card. This will help in evaluating if you really need the purchase or more time to do a price comparison. Ensure that you develop a habit of saving up instead of having a tendency to use credit cards; this will help in avoiding any interest on the cost price.

✔ Always limit the purchases that you do use your credit card. In situations whereby you run out of cash, chances are that you will end up using your credit card even if you cannot even afford the purchase and paying the balance. Learn to resist from using your credit cards when making any purchases that you know you cannot afford and especially on this that you do not need.

✔   Develop a habit of saving regularly. Open a savings account and ensure that you deposit money regularly; you can do it daily, weekly, or monthly depending on your income. This will definitely help in developing a healthier financial habit. Another better way will be to set up a plan that the funds are automatically credited to your account. That will help reduce the responsibility of reminding yourself to do that all the time.

✔   If you need to be a good manager when it comes to money, ensure that you practice it all the time. Plan when you intend to make a purchase and always buy what you can afford. When you make it a routine and a daily habit, it will be easier to manage money and the better for your finances.

Money Market Mistakes

To be successful in your investment in the money market, you need to ask yourself several questions/statements:

- Do you have an account for emergencies?
- The account that you have will be an investment
- That the funds you are setting aside will be useful soon.

When you decide to invest, you need to know that it is a risky venture and there are factors that you will need to consider first before any investment. For instance, when you decide to invest in a stock you need to know of factors like economic volatility. In the case of bonds, there are challenges like interest rates and inflationary risks. For a brave investor, leaning on a money market account will be a brave move. This is because they are known for safekeeping for the money. There are several mistakes when it comes to money market:

✔ The mistake that most investors make is thinking that money market accounts are the same as money market funds. They are financial instruments that have distinctive differences. Most people know of the money market fund as a mutual fund, the main characteristics are low returns and risks for every investment. They invest their funds in liquid assets for example cash. When invested in debt securities they have higher returns and ratings and mature in a shorter time. Most investors make the mistake and think that their money is safer in the money market, but that is not the same as with money market funds.

✔ Most people who are in investment believe that the money that they have in the money market is safe. The biggest mistake that they make is thinking that they are even safer from investments. Another belief is that, it better to have a lower interest rate with money in the bank than no interest at all. Most investors do not know the exposure they are in regarding inflation. This is the main reason that funds that are in the money market will not beat inflation. A good example is when the inflation rate is low than the interest that is claimed. Investors would know that, even though they believe the money market is safe, they are not safe from inflation.

✔ When in investment, you always need to know how to strike the right balance. Most of the time, the money market is influenced by inflation changes and rates. When you have such an investment, do not be tempted to input higher capital. They need a higher minimum balance as compared to the normal savings accounts. The normal account needs to be in operation for at least one year and have a higher amount of capital. When you have anything more than that, then it will be sitting their idle and it will lose value.

✔ Most investors like using money as their safety blanket. They believe that when they hold onto their money, it will be the best approach for any investment. This is not true especially when it is about savings whether in their money market or standard savings. It is not right to have your money exposed to uncertainty and any risk. This is one of the reasons why investors are afraid to invest and they would rather stay with their cash.

✔ To be a good investor, you need to know about asset diversification. When you are dealing with cash that is no different at all; this is because most people believe that cash is not an asset. You need to know that from the basics of finance and accounting, cash is known as a current asset. When you decide to hold on cash, ensure you do not hold more than $200k. It is not a coincidence to find any ordinary investor who has several bank accounts, in order to secure their cash. They have an approach to divide money or cash into three categories and that is a useful thing. The first one is to ensure that you have some money set aside for at least 3 years that is considered a shorter period. Around 4 to 10 years as the average timeframe and above 10 years as the longest timeframe. This is what will help the investors to know how long they can time their projects, how much is needed, and what will be saved in the end. This approach is important because it will also help in knowing about all the risks.

The best advice is to ensure that you invest in investments that are in the long-term and on lower risks. These will include investments like bonds, treasury bonds, life insurance, and annuity. You will need to know of the options that will help to avoid losing money value, avoiding any risks and the different ways about cash diversification. You can make use of the different trading and investment tools that will help in giving more returns instead of money market accounts. You need to look for investments that will help in creating more returns in a shorter time than the longer timeframe.

- Any investor needs to know that the reason for the money market is to hold money. When you have your money in just one place, you will not have any earnings or benefits; you need to move the money around. You will need to get more information on the different options and invest more. You should also know that money market accounts are not to be considered as long-term investments. The main reason is that they are subject to high interest rates than what is charged on a normal savings account. Hence not the reason to consider it a long-term investment.

✔ You should not be enticed to look for accounts that offer interest rates as a promotion. The reason is the interests are bound to change after some time.

Budgeting Apps

As an investor, you need to know that, with the tough economic times you need to know the best way to invest in the financial market. And when you become successful and start making money, you need to look for apps that will in managing your money. Thanks to technology all, those apps are easily available and easy to download. They can be downloaded and installed on tablets and smartphones; hence you can use them anytime and anywhere you are due to portability. The apps help is keeping you on track regarding the way you spend and how you spend.

✔ MINT:

Mint can be downloaded as an app or used as a website; it is in the budgeting and investment category. It is compatible with iOS, Web, Windows 8, and Android. It is more of a budgeting app and it will still help in managing your money. It has a feature whereby you can categorize and customize all your expenses and transactions. It has the ability to synchronize all your transactions from investments, bank accounts, and credit cards. They have a reminder feature for all your pending bills and this helps to avoid any lateness in bill payment that should be very convenient for any investor. All you need to do is set up a free account and then include all your financial details. This will then give a breakdown anytime an activity happens and you will be able to get a report.

✓ **Good Budget:**

This app uses the envelope concept, when you sign up you are given 10 free envelopes when you are on standard subscription. When you have an upgrade to Plus, you will then be charged a monthly charge of $6, and then you will have unlimited envelopes. The concept works in a way that, when your envelope is empty, you are not able to shop or spend any money. The other alternative is that you can move money among envelopes; this is because the app has the flexibility to use a common budget. You can share the budget with other people, the app is compatible with iPhone and all android devices.

- **Dollar Bird:**

This app also helps in money management; it manages future expenses and will remind you when you have payment dues. To set up and activate is free and it has additional premium features. Your budget will be broken down in a calendar form and your pending expenses will be visible. You have the chance to have all your transactions in categories that are color-coded and they will keep on adding up as you have repeated transactions. When you check on your utility bill and paycheck, they will be displayed there. You will be able to see all your current balance. What you can spend and still be on a budget. The main setback is that it does not synchronize will your bank accounts. The problem is you will need to manually enter all the transactions. The app is available for iOS users, Android, and the web. You will have the privilege to know about your income, expenses, and cash flow.

- **EXPENSIFY:**

This is considered an app and tool that is used to report expenses, track all receipts, and all the expenses that you have. The main advantage is that it helps in quick data entry and saves a lot of time doing data entry. You will have the opportunity to make all the entries in one click. This app is available for Android and iOS users, you will do all the capturing automatically and using OCR; this is a smart scan. All your reports are available by taking one picture and they are all uploaded and completed within a click. When you submit your expense, they get reimbursed faster and approvals are done very fast. When you use the app, you will be able to track all your expenses, categorize all of them, know the cost of all. All the expenses are consolidated and synchronized.

Chapter 9   Swing Trading Strategies

Like with any other version of trading, there are various strategies that you can use throughout your trading career. While most people like to stick to one or two strategies, which means they have to find financial instruments that work with their chosen strategies, other traders tend to go from one strategy to the next. However, as a beginner, it is best to realize that you should stick with one strategy as this will help you continue to learn about swing trading and how the stock market works in general. Of course, as you continue to build your trading knowledge and become more comfortable with swing trading, you can look into other strategies. While I cannot discuss all of the strategies in this chapter, I am discussing some of the most important and popular ones.

Trend Following

No matter what strategy you decide to use, you will need to make sure that you understand how to read charts and trend lines. You will use these tools in order to help guide you towards the best time to make your move to buy and sell a stock. When it comes to following a trend, there are a lot of details; such as what the opening price was, the highest price, the lowest price, and the closing price. You will analyze the trend over a period of time, how long depends on your personal preference. Through your analysis, you will start to notice a pattern in the trend line. This is the pattern that you will follow when you decide to take on a stock, see if your strategy will work for the stock, or what strategy to use.

The factors that you will look at when trend following are:

Price of the Stock

The price of the stock is one of the most important features that you will pay attention to. This doesn't just mean the price of the stock at that moment, such as what you would pay in order to purchase the stock. Even though the current price is the most important price, you will want to pay attention to all of the prices that you see for every day that you take into your analysis. For example, if you decide to look at the historical context of the last two months, you will look at about 60 days of stock pricing in order to help you find a trend. This means that you will look at the opening price for each of these days, the closing price, the highest price, and the lowest price. You will want to look at these prices in detail and in general. In a sense, this means that you will look at the larger image and the smaller pieces that make up the larger image.

Managing Your Money

Money management is thought to be one of the trickiest parts of trading. When it comes to managing your money, you want to make sure that you don't have too much money as it can give you a bigger loss. However, if you have too little money for the stock, then you aren't able to reach the full benefits when you make the trade. This is another time in swing trading when you want to find the best spot in order to make the trade.

One of the biggest tips to help you figure out how much money to put towards a stock is by evaluating the risks associated with the stock. You will be able to do this through any strategy that you will use and various other factors that are part of your trading plan.

Rules and Guidelines

One of the most important factors to remember when you are looking towards your trend line and thinking of making a trade. These rules are not only the guidelines that you will receive as you start to learn the swing trading technique, they are also the rules that you will set for yourself. For example, if you decide that your stop-loss price is going to be $10.00 lower than the price you bought the stock from, you will want to make sure that you follow this guideline.

One of the biggest reasons you need to make sure that you are following your guidelines is because the more consistent you are with your trading, the more likely you are to become successful. Furthermore, you will want to make sure that you follow the guidelines as they will help you to think systematically when it comes to making decisions. While you might find yourself turning back to your trading plan and guidelines consistently as a beginner, the more you follow the same procedures, the more you will focus on them as a way in making sure you are following the steps instead of needing them more for direct reference on where to go and what to do next. In a sense, trading will start to become more natural to you, which is a great strength when you are analyzing trend lines.

Diversity

Diversity is one of the more popular controversies when it comes to trading. While some traders feel you need to have great diversity, which is a variety of stocks, in your portfolio others feel that this isn't as important. In reality, the more serious you want to be with your trading, the more you will focus on diversity. However, this isn't always true when it comes to investors. But, as stated before, investing and trading are two different career paths in the stock market.

You can look at diversity as what is the right feature for you. You might find that you don't need to have a large diversity because you are a part-time swing trader or you have a specific target that you focus on. However, you might also find that the more diversity you have, the better-rounded you feel as a trader. You might find that diversity is helping you learn more about investing in general.

Always Note the Risk

Another important factor to pay attention to when you are looking into trend following is how much risk is involved if you decide to take on the financial instrument you are looking at. When you are looking at the risk, you always have to pay attention to your guidelines and your trading plan. These two factors will help you decide if you should take on the stock due to the risk it carries or not. It is important to remember you need to stick to the risk level you are comfortable with. Even if you think that this stock could give you good rewards, this doesn't mean that you should agree to take on the financial instrument if you are uncomfortable with the risk.

This also doesn't mean that you can't increase your risk level as time goes on. You just want to make sure that you build your confidence and comfort level with risk as your risk grows. Furthermore, as you get more knowledgeable with swing trading, it might be a good thing to slowly increase your risk when it comes to taking on stocks. It's always good to grow in many directions as a trader, including with risk.

Trend following tends to be one of the most popular techniques when it comes to trading because it has a high success rate, providing you understand where the trend line is heading. Of course, you should always remember that the stock market can take drastic turns and no one can truly predict the future. This means, even if you analyze the trend lines to the best degree, you will still have some risk involved as the trend line could differ a bit from what you originally thought.

Using Options As A Strategy

We have already discussed what options are; however, one factor I did not discuss is how options are usually seen as a strategy when it comes to trading. Because you are able to set up an agreement which gives you the option to buy or sell the stock later, you are technically strategizing the right time to take the next step in the future.

One of the biggest ways to do this is through analyzing the various charts that you see for your stock. In fact, you will focus a lot on technical analysis, which is something I will discuss later. You will focus on the historical charts of the stock as this will give you a time-frame for when you will want to take the next step.

Options are known to be a great strategy if you are looking for leverage, which is when you increase a return on a trade through borrowed money. It is important that you need to make sure you will only use this strategy if it will help you to receive more of a profit. In fact, this is one of the most important factors of choosing a strategy. You have to make sure that it is going to help you gain a profit and decrease your risks.

Short Interest

Many experienced traders state that beginners should not take part in the short interest strategy as it tends to be more of a guessing game than other strategies. When you focus on the short interest strategy, you will compare the number of short shares to the number of floating shares.

This is a great strategy to learn as a swing trader because it can show when the stock market is about to go into bearish conditions, which means that the stock prices will start to go down. Furthermore, short interest can also warn you about short squeezing.

Pay Attention To The Float

One of the best ways that you can tell if a trade is going to help you is through a technique known as float. Basically, a float is the total number of shares that a trader will find in public sharing. This can become very helpful because, if you have the right size of float, you can see higher profits.

However, this is also the trick when it comes to the float strategy. There tends to be a fine line between having a massive float and having a float that will give you the best profits. The reason why a massive float, which would be too many shares, can cause you to lose capital instead of increasing your profits is because if you have a huge float, the price won't move as quickly. However, if you have a smaller amount of shares in your float, then you will find that the price moves a bit higher, of course this gives you a larger profit. With this said, you also don't want to have too little shares in your float. If this happens, then you won't be able to make much of a profit either as this can stop your float from increasing in price.

Breakout And Breakdown Strategies

When you focus on the breakout strategy, you are looking at the history of your stock's trend line in a microscopic fashion. What I mean by this is you will be focusing on what the trend has done over the past few days. When you are looking at the trend line, you will see every time the price has gone up and down. Stock prices are almost constantly changing throughout the day, which is what the trend line shows. Every now and then, you will notice in the trend line that you have a several high points and several low points. These high points indicated the highest prices of the stock and the lowest points show the lowest prices.

The biggest difference between the breakout strategy compared to the breakdown strategy is the condition of the market. If you notice that the stock has been going on an upward trend for a while, you will use the breakout strategy. However, if you notice that the trend shows the price has been decreasing over time, you will use the breakdown strategy.

Of course, for both strategies, there is that specific spot you need to try in order to gain your best profit. The best spot to make your next move will depend on the pattern of the trend.

News Playing

As you know by now, one of the most important parts of your day is your pre-trading portion. This is one of the first things you will do once you start your day. You will want to do this before you start trading; however, you will probably be checking out the stock market so you can see the changes in your stocks and any target stocks that you are watching.

However, one of the most important parts of this part of the day is reading the news that happened over night. This is important because you need to know what news is going to affect what stock, especially if you own the stock. You should always make note that any type of news can affect the pricing of financial instruments. For example, if you read that a company donated a large amount of money towards a nonprofit organization, people might be more likely to invest in that stock. However, if you read any negative news about a company, you will find the stock price going down because people are selling their shares.

But, you need to remember the trick of keeping your emotions out of the stock market. While News Playing is a strategy which is used all across the board when it comes to the stock market, for example all traders and investors use this strategy, it is important to remember that you should never make a decision to sell or take on a stock because of your emotions. I won't go much more into this because I discuss how your emotions can be a risk factor in the stock market in another chapter, but it is also a big part of News Playing that you have to look out for.

You always want to make sure that you think logically when you are making a decision to buy or sell a stock. Even if you find you hold a stock where the price is dropping due to negative news, you want to make sure you continue to follow your trading plan instead of going on your emotions. Therefore, you should only focus on selling the stock if the price drops to your stop-loss price. You also should not hold on to a stock for longer than you originally planned, even if they are the center of a positive news story. While you can be a little flexible when the price continues to rise, at least in swing trading, you don't want to hold on to the stock for longer than a swing trader should. You always have to keep the time-frame in mind.

Conclusion

This book should have been able to guide you through everything there is to know about the stock market and swing trade. I wish every question you had has been adequately answered by this beautiful book here. You should, by this point, know whether you would use swing trade in the process of investing in the stock market. The essential things should be ready at your fingertips and ready for usage at any point you decide to trade.

Swing trade and its aspects have been figured out in this book. Swing trade has been seen to take up a little time in the stock market. It is seen as a quick, swift, and easy way to make a profit. Most traders who have a short time in their hands use this. Something else that has been mentioned in the characteristics of a swing trade. These are the basic things that bring about swing trade to be there. They are what make swing trade. These also help to differentiate swing trade from the other types of trading that exist in the stock market.

There is also the fact about technical analysis and fundamental analysis. These two types of analysis help to look at how the stock market is operating. They help to see if you get into the market right now. You will earn some profit, or you will get loses. The technical analysis helps to look into past trades and how the trends of the market have been in recent years. As for fundamental analysis, one can look at the outside factors that affect the stock market. One does not need to look into the market.

You should also understand what simulation trading is and how important it is to make sure you complete this type of trading before you start trading for money. You should also not only understand risks which are associated in swing trading but also have an idea on how to decrease these risks once you start swing trading. Of course, this is one reason you want to make sure to practice simulation trading at first. As stated before, simulation trading will help you make sure that you understand the risks and the strategies which are associated with swing trading.

By now you should not only clearly understand what swing trading is, but also what the average time fame is for a swing trader. You should be able to remember the 11 commandments of swing trading, techniques, what the right mindset is when you are trading, know a variety of tips to help you get on your way, and also understand the many mistakes that other swing traders have made.

Furthermore, you should be able to explain how a day will go for a full-time swing trader, be able to explain the two different types of stock market conditions, and the art of short selling.

On top of all the information you need to know about being a swing trader, you also know how to get started with researching as much information as possible. On top of this, you have learned tips to help you become a better researcher, so you can gain the most out of your research time. It is important to keep these tips in mind as you will need to used them throughout your career. On top of this, you can also add your own tips, which will become useful when you begin to help other beginner swing traders in the next few years.

www.ingramcontent.com/pod-product-compliance
Lightning Source LLC
Chambersburg PA
CBHW070631220526
45466CB00001B/147